BR STEAM
IN COLOUR

COLIN BOOCOCK

BR STEAM IN COLOUR

1948-1968

LONDON
IAN ALLAN LTD

Dedication

This book is dedicated to my parents, whose support in my formative years enabled my railway enthusiasm, and subsequently my railway career, to flourish.

Acknowledgements

There are doubtless many collections of excellent colour slides of the railway scene stored in numerous lofts and cupboards around the country. In such circumstances they serve little purpose, and run the risk of being lost to posterity when a photographer moves on.

Fortunately, there exists in Britain a service which brings together the best pictures from such collections and makes them available to railway enthusiasts the world over. Colour-Rail's current catalogue lists over 3,000 slides of railway interest, many of them historic or even unique in the subjects they cover. Duplicates of these slides are available for railway enthusiasts to purchase, subject to the national law of copyright. The quality of these duplicates can be judged from the many Colour-Rail slides used in this book, all of which are based on duplicate slides. This is a result of Colour-Rail's undertaking to slide owners that their precious originals will remain in the safe hands of Colour-Rail and their copiers, and will never be loaned to publishers or printers under any circumstances.

I have been privileged to be given the opportunity of dipping into the Colour-Rail collection. This has enabled this superb selection of pictures to be assembled. In doing this I have only been able to skim the surface of what is available!

Readers who wish to know more about the services offered by Colour-Rail should write for a catalogue to: 5 Treacher's Close, Chesham, Bucks HP5 2HD. (The catalogue is priced at £2 at the time of writing, but interested readers should first check advertisements in the monthly magazines for the current price.)

Credit

The picture credited to the late W. H. Foster has been made available through Colour-Rail by the trustees of the Lancashire & Yorkshire Railway Saddletanks Fund.

Half-title page:
Carrying the distinctive headboard of the 'Atlantic Coast Express', Bulleid 'West Country' Pacific No 34036 *Westward Ho!* takes water at the turntable at Padstow, with the estuary of the River Camel in the background.
B. J. Swain/Colour-Rail BRS427

Title page:
The LMS, and later BR, built some Class 5s with Caprotti poppet valve gear in an attempt further to improve their economy and performance. One of these, No 44753, was caught by the camera in February 1963 near Orton Bridge plodding up-grade with a heavy freight.
M. Chapman/Colour-Rail BRM433

First published 1986
Reprinted 1988

ISBN 0 7110 1671 2

Published by Ian Allan Ltd, Shepperton, Surrey; and printed by Chorley & Pickersgill Ltd, Leeds LS15 8AL

Front cover:
Double blastpipes and chimneys together with higher temperature superheat put new life into the ex-GWR 'King' class 4-6-0s. No 6019 *King Henry V* scatters the contents of the water troughs at Goring as it speeds towards Paddington with the up 'Red Dragon' in March 1961.
T. B. Owen/Colour-Rail BRW389

Back cover, top:
In the bleak countryside of the Scottish highlands, ex-Caledonian Railway 0-4-4T No 55217 waits with the branch train at Killin in May 1959.
W. J. V. Anderson/Colour-Rail SC133

Back cover, bottom:
Adams 'O2' class 0-4-4T No 30200 is seen with the 4.40pm Padstow-Bodmin North service near Grogley Halt in September 1960. *P. W. Gray/Colour Rail BRS252*

CONTENTS

The power of a BR Standard '9F' 2-10-0 is epitomised by this view of No 92058 hammering over Ais Gill with a long southbound freight, one year before the end of steam on BR. *Colour-Rail BRM115*

PREFACE
Steam's Glory

It was the sight of a steam locomotive in action that drew so many people into the railway enthusiast community. Lifetimes of devotion to railways resulted from encounters with steam engines; such was the impression of power, of aesthetic form, and of sound engineering. Indeed, surely the steam locomotive represented the ultimate combination in one machine of the art and science of mechanical engineering.

That this was so, is clear because the steam railway engine epitomised the old adage: 'If it looks right, it is right!' History has many instances where the ugly performed less well than the handsome. Compare the performance of the ill-proportioned 'A2' Pacific with the 'A3' or 'A4'; the 'Aberdare' with the '43XX'; the LMS '2P' with a 'T9'; the LNER 'L1' with a BR 2-6-4T. Even so, beauty is in the eye of the beholder, a cliché that was never so true as when applied to steam traction. Controversy rages still over the appearance of Bulleid's 'Q1' 0-6-0, thought by some to be ugly and by others to have a certain plain attractiveness. Many have affection for the simple form of the LNER 'B1' 4-6-0.

How else can one explain the almost universal adoration of all things Great Western? The GW's fleet of engines lacked visual variety and was technically 'safe' rather than up-to-date, but their embellishment with copper and brass decorations set them on pedestals in many men's hearts. Yet the LNER Gresley Pacifics had set new standards in performance as a result of that great engineer's humble acceptance that Chapelon of France could teach a few things, and the LMS pushed ahead with technical developments which extended intervals between repairs and reduced running costs. And even the relatively small Southern Railway had gone further with devices such as steel fireboxes and electric lighting on its technically extraordinary Pacifics.

So steam's glory is expressed in many ways according to one's point of view. It could be the sight of a streamlined 'A4' streaking across the flat Yorkshire plain, or the sound of a 'Duchess' pounding up Camden bank. Maybe the piercing whistle of an LNER 2-6-0 echoing around the mountains near Glenfinnan struck the imagination. Perhaps one was stirred by the steady grind of a 'WD' 2-8-0 hauling stone away from the Derbyshire Peak District, or by the towering billow of steam and smoke that exploded from a Bulleid Pacific as it lost its feet on trying to start its train.

There were, however, those to whom steam engines were less than glorious beasts. Have you ever had to fire a leaky 'H15' 4-6-0 on a heavy Feltham freight in coldest winter? Have your face, eyes, hair, hands, indeed most of you, emerged soot black from a smokebox after cleaning choked boiler fire tubes? Was it your back which ached after lying in a Bulleid 4-6-2's oil bath while you angled yourself to insert the circlips that kept the chain driven valve gear's pins in place? Could you have lived in a house opposite a large engine shed and breathed the smoke-laden atmosphere which blew across from the host of engines being lit up on a Sunday evening ready for next day's services? Or do you, as a passenger, remember that in early British Railways days we did not wear our best clothes when travelling, for fear of getting them marked with the coal dust that penetrated the rolling stock of those years?

Most of us look back in nostalgia, through rose-tinted spectacles, fondly recalling the good moments: the sparkle of Brunswick green paint, the brilliant white steam cloud, the majestic driving wheels, the proud nameplates bearing names of grandeur, the clang of the shovel in the firehole door, the hiss of the steam sanders, the steady acceleration of the deep exhaust beats as the train pulled away. All these are evocative reminders of the giants of steam.

This album is more than a collection of superb pictures journeying into nostalgia. Its chapters trace the path of steam's history during the turbulent first 20 years of the nationalised British Railways. In its pages, discussion ranges over the early decision to build large numbers of new steam locomotives; the success of the standard designs; improvements made to older types. Then the years of change are described, leading to steam's disappearance from the tracks.

If readers can recall their favourite types, remember their happiest journeys, or just wallow in pleasant memories while turning over these pages, this book will have succeeded as a memento of steam's glory.

In days of old there used to be a local push-pull train which operated between Craigendoran and Arrochar at the southern end of the West Highland line. On a summer's day in 1959 it was handled by ex-North British Class C15 4-4-2T 67460, pictured here at Garelochhead.
Don Beecroft/Colour-Rail SC385

On the St Ives branch line in Cornwall, GW 2-6-2T No 4564 arrives at Carbis Bay towards the end of the 1961 holiday season. *P. W. Gray/Colour-Rail BRW264*

Above:

A happy feature of the last decade of steam on BR was the use in traffic of early locomotives repainted in pre-Grouping (pre-1923) liveries. The restoration was done on the understanding that when the engines were not required for special workings they would be used in normal service. Thus the appearance of 'Jones Goods' 4-6-0 No 103 on a mixed train near Strome Ferry on the Kyle of Lochalsh line was not unusual in 1959! *Derek Cross/Colour-Rail P79*

Left:

The most numerous class of steam locomotives in Britain was the ex-GW Class 57XX 0-6-0 pannier tank design, used variously for shunting, freight and local passenger duties. This 1958 view shows No 3600 running round the branch passenger train at Moretonhampstead.
T. B. Owen/Colour-Rail BRW649

Left:

The rural railway by-way has almost disappeared since this photograph was taken in 1957 of ex-Great Eastern Class D16/3 4-4-0 No 62596 at Gunton with the 9.00am from Gorleston to York. We don't even stack corn like that now!
E. Alger/Colour-Rail BRE564

'Rebuilt Scot' No 46108 *Seaforth Highlander* makes a fine picture as it heads an Aberdeen-Manchester train near Howgill. *A. E. R. Cope/Colour-Rail BRM473*

Ex-works 'Castle' class 4-6-0 No 7022 *Hereford Castle* working the 6.10pm Goodrington-Plymouth meets 2-6-2T No 4561 on a local freight near Aller Junction in July 1960.

P. W. Gray/Colour-Rail BRW 189

INTRODUCTION
A Future for Steam?

'Is there a future for steam?' In 1948 it was logical to reach the conclusion that steam traction had a future on British Railways. The argument goes thus.

The four main constituents of BR survived World War 2 with large fleets of steam locomotives totalling over 20,000. While admiring the former independent railways' latest products, young railway engine cleaners also had to attend to locomotives which were as old as were their grandfathers. The newly constituted British Railways could, however, draw on virtually no history of main line diesel traction and had limited diesel railcar experience. Apart from the Southern Region's third rail network, electrification had been limited to some suburban lines in large provincial cities. Money was not in plentiful supply.

With these factors in mind (and with the undoubted advantage of hindsight!) we can envisage a list of options which might have been considered for rejuvenating the locomotive fleet:

Electrify main lines.
Dieselise secondary routes.
Build diesels for shunting.
Design and build new standard steam locomotives.
Adopt as standard the best existing steam types from the 'Big Four' railways.
Continue building Regional types in their current proliferation.

In considering these and other options, the Railway Executive would have recognised that the postwar shortage of capital would preclude widespread electrification at that time. Limited experience of diesel traction in this country would have made general dieselisation a high risk policy. At a time when action was urgent, risks had to be minimised.

So, seen from the situation in which BR found itself in 1948, a decision to continue building steam locomotives would have appeared logical. At the same time, the use of diesels for shunting was already established, and new construction of diesel shunters could be encouraged to the limit of available supply, supplemented by steam types to meet foreseen demands.

What, then, should be the policy for new construction of steam locomotives? Again, circumstances in 1948 should be considered. Each of the Regions had production lines of former designs in full swing at their main workshops. To design and introduce new standard types for BR would take time. It would also take time to test and select standard types from among the former railways' designs. To impose these on other Regions and re-jig their works production to construct and repair unfamiliar types could have been counter-productive.

So logic indicated that BR should, in the short term, go on building existing types in the Regions' workshops and at contractors, at least until a longer-term policy could be established. In fact, an early decision was taken to design and introduce as soon as possible a range of new standard steam locomotives of low-risk, simple designs that would meet all Regions' future motive power requirements. These standard steam types would have lower maintenance costs, would in time displace the Regional designs, and would in their turn eventually be displaced by hoped-for future electrification of main lines supported by selective dieselisation of other routes when enough experience had been gained of the new types of traction.

Meanwhile, the LNER and Southern Railway in particular had bequeathed BR such an array of old fashioned, outdated engines on branch line, shunting and light mixed traffic duties that an interim policy was adopted in these cases. Modern, LMS-designed locomotives were delivered in some numbers to these areas until equivalent BR standard designs were available. In particular one recalls the Southern Region's use of Fairburn 2-6-4Ts, built at Brighton works to replace pre-Grouping (1923) designs, and the spread of Ivatt 2-6-0s into the North Eastern Region and on to the Midland & Great Northern section of the Eastern.

From 1951, in a remarkably short timescale, appeared the new BR Standard types. They met their principal objectives well, and some were indeed brilliant performers. Others needed improvements which are documented later in this book.

By the early 1950s, motive power policy was beginning to evolve towards fundamental change. Firstly, the advantages of diesel railcars had been grasped, and from 1953 these appeared in large numbers, putting into question the futures of some of the recently built branch line steam classes. When the 1955 Modernisation Plan was announced by the Conservative government of the day, the *Sunday Express* ran the banner headline: 'The End of the Steam Train!' In 1957 came the pilot main line diesels, followed, more quickly than had been planned, by large builds of new diesel locomotives for general main line mixed traffic use.

These new orders for diesels sounded the death knell for new steam locomotive construction, though it took a couple of years to stop building steam for good. Certainly, the Modernisation Plan did not herald the immediate cessation of construction of steam locomotives. Indeed some works, such as Swindon, produced new steam and diesel locomotives alongside one another for some years. History records that No 92220 *Evening Star* left Swindon Works in 1960, to bring new steam construction for British Railways to its end.

Technically, BR steam locomotive development had not stood still during these years. Improvements had been made to several types, including favourites like the 'Castles' and 'A3s', and major projects such as the rebuilding of the Bulleid Pacifics had been undertaken.

However, a major event, foreshadowed by another newspaper's headline, 'Dr Beeching's Pill', was to change the life-span of the entire steam fleet, and was even to change the prospects of some of the diesels as well. BR's chairman, Dr Richard Beeching (later Lord Beeching) began asking questions about the economic size of the railway system, and got some controversial answers. In the years following 1962, many miles of under-utilised railway, duplicate routes and lightly used stations and goods yards were closed. The demand for locomotives was suddenly cut back, and the wholesale scrapping of steam traction which followed has no comparison in British railway history, not even with the Great Western's withdrawal of its broad gauge engines, itself also a late reaction to inevitable market forces. Thus, the latest '9Fs' which were new in 1960 had all gone by 1968. Bulleid Pacifics, on which considerable sums had been spent in rebuilding, had no more than 10, and sometimes as little as four years to recover these costs by savings in maintenance and fuel consumption. And even some diesels which were new in the late 1950s had found their way to scrapyards by the late 1960s.

In 1967, British Rail had only one main line still using steam to haul express passenger trains. The Southern had planned its Bournemouth electrification to be completed in 1967, and on 9 July that year the last express steam train, hauled by a Bulleid Pacific, reached its Waterloo. The next year, railway enthusiasts went on pilgrimages to places such as Carnforth and Lostock Hall to witness the last months of steam haulage of freight and local passenger services on the London Midland Region, and on BR. Familiar 'Black 5s', '8Fs', and BR 4-6-0s clanked across the hills with their loads.

Then suddenly it was all over.

One of the last 'Jubilees' in service, No 45562 *Alberta* makes a fine sight passing Grayrigg with the 'Border Countryman' special in February 1967. *A. E. R. Cope/Colour-Rail BRM478*

Stanier 'Black 5' No 45130 stands at Bangor, North Wales, in 1956 with a down express.   *J. H. Moss/Colour-Rail BRM816*

Above:
The tranquility of the rural railway is portrayed by Class 14XX 0-4-2T No 1450 propelling a single auto-coach from Bampton to Exeter, as recently as 1963.
T. B. Owen/Colour-Rail BRW456

Left:
The grace of steam is illustrated by this 1959 view of spotless Great Western 4-6-0 No 7811 *Dunley Manor* near Bow Street on the up 'Cambrian Coast Express'.
T. B. Owen/Colour-Rail BRW552

The massive variety of pre-Grouping locomotives ensured that many were confined to their home localities. At Craigellachie No 62262, a 4-4-0 of the former Great North of Scotland Railway, is in charge of a freight for Aviemore in August 1954. *E. S. Russell/Colour-Rail SC165*

The Great Western 'Kings' did excellent work on the Birmingham line. 4-6-0 No 6012 *King Edward VI* was photographed near Beaconsfield in April 1962 heading the 11.00am Birmingham Snow Hill-Paddington. *P. Mullett/Colour-Rail BRW330*

Top:
Rebuilt 'Royal Scot' 4-6-0 No 46142 *The York & Lancaster Regiment* **scuttles through the Lune gorge on the West Coast main line in June 1963.**
M. Chapman/Colour-Rail BRM567

Above:
The hobby of train spotting reached its zenith in the 1960s; it dropped significantly after the end of steam in 1968. A new generation of modern traction enthusiasts has lately revived the hobby, and has resumed the practice of gathering at the lineside to watch their favourites, such as these spotters were doing back in 1960 as Stanier 'Princess Royal' 4-6-2 No 46207 *Princess Arthur of Connaught* **passed Bushey with the up 'Ulster Express'.**
T. B. Owen/Colour-Rail BRM666

Above:
In east Lancashire, Stanier LMS 2-6-4T No 42460 enters Colne with a stopping train from Blackburn.
G. Warnes/Colour-Rail BRM583

Below:
Heavy summer holiday trains in the West Country needed two engines to be able to surmount the banks. Ex-GW 4-6-0s Nos 7813 *Freshford Manor* and 6832 *Brockton Grange* head 16 coaches from Newquay across the lattice viaduct at Largin in September 1958.
T. B. Owen/Colour-Rail BRW445

Top:
The Southern's 'Lord Nelson' 4-6-0s performed competently if not outstandingly on the Bournemouth expresses and Southampton boat trains. One of these popular machines brings a Bournemouth-Waterloo train into Winchester.
Colin Boocock

Above:
In this busy evening scene at Perth, 'Rebuilt Scot' No 46166 *London Rifle Brigade* has arrived with a down express and Class 5 No 44997 waits to take over for the assault of the Highland main line towards Inverness. A former Caledonian tank simmers by the side of the station.
W. J. V. Anderson/Colour-Rail SC123

ONE

EXPRESS INHERITANCE

It is a brave man who can stand up amid a railway gathering and pronounce definitively which class of top express locomotive was the best inherited by British Railways in 1948. The 'A4s', 'Duchesses'. 'Merchant Navies' and 'Kings' all had their individual best features.

Foremost in terms of maximum speed were the LNER 'A4s', with *Mallard* holding the world speed record of 126mph. Sir Nigel Gresley had gifted his streamlined 4-6-2s with scientifically profiled aerofoil curves to reduce air resistance at high speed, a powerful, free-steaming boiler for sustained high output, and large cross-section steam and exhaust passages to ensure efficient steam distribution and exhaust release. His conjugated inside valve gear, subject to overrun when worn, and the propensity for the inside big end to overheat were the only significant faults of an intelligently evolved design.

The LMS matched the 'A4' with a slightly bigger brute with four cylinders which produced a theoretically greater tractive effort. The 'Duchesses' were at least as well suited to hard slog as they were to high speed, but nonetheless one of the streamlined version was once pushed to 114mph near Crewe. In the 1948 locomotive exchanges, when the best engines of each of the former railways were tested on each others' routes, the LMS '8P' Pacifics recorded the most economical performances, though not the most startling running. The 'Duchesses' and their sister 'Cities' performed reliably, hauling enormous length trains on the West Coast main line to Glasgow over Shap and Beattock summits, sometimes reaching as far north as Perth. They were Britain's biggest Pacifics.

The Southern Railway also had heavy loads to pull over very difficult, hilly roads such as those from London to Dover and to Exeter via Salisbury. Bulleid's provision for the SR of the 'Merchant Navy' class 4-6-2s presented that railway with a class of very high performers, capable of exceptionally high boiler outputs, speeds of over 100mph (with 6ft 2in wheels!) and many modern features. His steel fireboxes proved to be a highly successful feature. With controlled water treatment they were very easy on firebox maintenance. Drivers liked the enclosed cabs and electric lighting and the thoughtful placing of the controls within easy reach of the driving position. The locomotives'

countless mechanical innovations, such as chain-driven valve gear in an oil bath, flat plate smokebox and fabricated chimney, steam reverse and steam-powered firehole door, seriously reduced the reliability of these handsome machines. The valve gear in particular used to overrun and cut-off late at high speeds, a major cause of heavy fuel and water consumption (and the cause of the myth that they were very free running at high speed!). Nonetheless their running was frequently brilliant, and particularly so in the 1948 exchanges where economy was sacrificed against high power outputs.

The Great Western had relied on its 'King' class 4-6-0s since 1927. Very handsome indeed, and extremely powerful for a 4-6-0 design, with normal loads they edged into the performance league represented by the other railways' largest Pacific types. The 'Kings' were, after all, the oldest '8P' locomotives and their narrow fireboxes must have been a limitation to absolute maximum power. Their greater width across the cylinders prevented their trial over more than the GW and LNER main lines in 1948, and the Pacifics really held the limelight at that time.

When British Railways had decided on standard colours to paint their stock, all these magnificent, inherited, top-link machines from the'Big Four' railways received a strong blue livery with black and white lining-out, overlaid on the tenders with the smart new lion-over-wheel emblem of BR. Coupled to red and cream coaches, these engines all looked superb, and attracted a great deal of admiration. Blue was a natural colour anyway for an 'A4'. It equally suited the air-smoothed 'Merchant Navy' and the bulk of a Stanier 'Duchess'. A blue 'King' was a novelty, certainly, in many opinions a handsome one, but diehard opinion preferred GWR Brunswick green!

Later, British Railways decided that the blue did not wear well (the author has no recollection of this actually being the case) and the locomotives were subsequently repainted in BR Brunswick green at their next overhaul. While the 'Kings' and 'Merchant Navies' still looked fine in green, the 'Duchesses' looked less strong and the 'A4s' partially lost their appeal.

Brunswick green had already been applied to the railways' other express engines, too, down through the lesser 4-6-2s ('A3s', 'A2s', 'West Countries') and the 4-6-0s as low as power class 5P. Thus the Southern's splendid 'King Arthurs' were green, and so were the 'B17s', 'Jubilees', rebuilt 'Royal Scots', 'Lord Nelsons' and 'Castles'.

The '7P' range was a mixed bunch of types, typified by the 'Castles', 'Lord Nelsons' and 'Royal Scots'. The 1948 exchanges pitted 'West Country' Pacifics as the Southern's entries in the mixed traffic range, but the smaller LMS 'Royal Scots' had to perform against the '8P' giants. In Scotland the SR's light Pacific amazed the locals with its haulage exploits over the Highland main line. On the SR these engines often deputised competently for their bigger 'Merchant Navy' sisters, though they suffered from most of the bigger engines' design difficulties.

The 'Castles' were the mainstay of Western Region main line services and performed with economy and distinction even when driven quite hard. They were more of a racehorse breed than a heavy haulage machine, and double-heading was very common on the steeper banks in the West.

The similarity in size between a 'Castle' and a 'Lord Nelson' is clearly evident. The 'Nelsons' were in many ways of sewing machine quality mechanically, and were extremely reliable. However, their very long fireboxes were difficult to fire successfully. Eastleigh depot men made well with them on Southampton boat trains as they were well suited to that depot's light-handed handling of its steeds. Demonstration of the heavy haulage ability of a 'Lord Nelson' however has had to wait until the 1980s and the preservation era! That is another story.

The LMS bequeathed to BR its large fleet of 'Royal Scots', still being rebuilt with taper boilers, a programme which BR went on to complete. The 'Royal Scots' had originally been built with an eye on the 'Lord Nelson' design for guidance. Why the 'Scots' needed rebuilding and the 'LNs' did not is a question few Derby men would answer, one fears! That is a particularly poignant point because the smaller 'Patriots' apparently performed satisfactorily (even though BR initially painted them black), and indeed the later 'Jubilee' 4-6-0s were barely distinguishable in the consistency of their performance. In good hands the 'Jubilees' put up some sparkling performances, particularly on the main line out of St Pancras. Heavy loads on that route demanded double heading however; the London Midland Region sorely needed bigger engines.

A big engine policy had already provided the LNER with a large fleet of Pacifics of 'A2', 'A3' and 'A4' types, and the 'A1' design appeared on the scene just after Nationalisation. (Indeed one newspaper was seen to comment that the first BR Standard engine had appeared!) Mr Peppercorn's three-cylinder simple Pacific was a splendid, basic machine, stronger than an 'A4' and without its mechanical weaknesses. The 'A1s' were indeed

handsome and worked heavy trains from King's Cross to Leeds, York and Newcastle with ease. The problems with the 'A2' 4-6-2s have been well documented elsewhere, but in reality their running could often match their larger-wheeled Peppercorn sisters. They found very useful employment particularly over Scotland's hilly main lines. The Gresley 'A3s' likewise put up fine performances, often only slightly inferior to the bigger machines.

However, the LNER had left a considerable tract of its territory with its express trains underpowered. The Great Eastern lines to Norwich and Cambridge had nothing bigger than the Gresley three-cylinder 'B17' 4-6-0s or their Thompson two-cylinder 'B2' equivalents to haul the express trains, which meant that speeds were not high, particularly on the difficult Norwich route. Equally, the Southern did not have enough Pacifics to cover all heavy trains, and many passengers to Ramsgate and Dover found their 12-coach trains headed by nothing bigger than a 'Schools' class 4-4-0. Even though these engines were the biggest 4-4-0s in Europe, and also were technically excellent and efficient engines, they were not big enough for much that they had to do, and timings on the Kent lines were slow in consequence. BR at first did not even think of them as being worthy of green livery. They were painted black, with LNW-style red, cream and grey lining, and when clean they looked very smart indeed; not an express livery though!

So British Railways' express inheritance was a group of highly competent top-link classes between which any logical choice was difficult, and a wide mixture of second and third range types (7P, 6P and 5P power classes), only a few of which were really modern and most of which had characteristics unsuitable for adoption as the basis for standard BR designs.

For example, neither the 'Castles' nor the 'Lord Nelsons' were modern designs. The 'Royal Scots' were no real match for the '7P' 4-6-2s which the Southern and LNER possessed. Yet the 'West Country' and 'Battle of Britain' class possessed Bulleid's engineering features, the 'A2s' sometimes rode indifferently and were strictly of main line route availability, and the 'A3' lineage dated from the Great Northern Railway's 'A1' class of 1922. Also, the 'King Arthur' and 'B17'/'B2' classes were completely outclassed by more modern mixed traffic types.

BR's perceived need therefore was for higher powered locomotives on the secondary main lines of Britain. How this need was eventually met emerges in later chapters.

Incidentally, the London Midland Region did solve the problem of the unsatisfactory appearance of 'Duchesses' in green. By adopting a maroon colour, reminiscent of the former LMS red, the looks of these great engines were transformed, as illustrations in this book testify.

The fastest steam locomotives to be inherited by British Railways were without doubt the Gresley 'A4' Pacifics. No 60008 *Dwight D. Eisenhower* shows off its curves while standing near the coaling plant at King's Cross depot.
P. Mullett/Colour-Rail BRE270

Above:

Gresley's 'A3' class were fine looking locomotives. No 60093 *Coronach* is seen in original form at Edinburgh at the head of a Waverley route express to Carlisle.
J. G. Wallace/Colour-Rail SC427

Left:

The Southern bequeathed the solid and reliable 'King Arthur' class 4-6-0s to British Railways, exemplified by No 30794 *Sir Ector de Maris*, photographed in January 1959 passing Pirbright Junction with a down Southampton Docks boat train. T. B. Owen/Colour-Rail BRS397

Left:

The Southern 'Schools' were the largest 4-4-0s in Europe. No 30927 *Clifton* leaves Dover under the white cliffs near Shakespeare tunnel with an up express in 1958. Electrification displaced these fine engines four years later. T. B. Owen/Colour-Rail BRS452

Top:
The fine appearance of Maunsell's four-cylinder 'Lord Nelson' class 4-6-0s is displayed by this view at Eastleigh depot of No 30863 *Lord Rodney.*   *Colin Boocock*

Above:
The handsome lines of ex-Great Western 'King' 4-6-0 No 6011 *King James I* (at Bath Spa in 1950) are emphasised by BR's early blue livery, illustrated in this rare colour slide. Most people preferred the former Brunswick green, to which BR reverted around 1950.
Kenneth Leech/Colour-Rail BRW329

Left:
The Thompson rebuilds of Gresley's 'P2' 2-8-2s into 'A2/2' class 4-6-2s were not entirely successful, and the locomotives were withdrawn from service early. Near the end of its life, No 60506 *Wolf of Badenoch* **was photographed in August 1959 on an up express near Eaton Wood.** *P. J. Hughes/Colour-Rail BRE256*

Left:
Crossing the river Clyde at Crawford in September 1964 is 'Rebuilt Scot' 4-6-0 No 46140 *The King's Royal Rifle Corps* **at the head of a down express.**
A. E. R. Cope/Colour-Rail SC220

Below:
The massive bulk of 'Princess Royal' 4-6-2 No 46208 *Princess Helena Victoria* **is dressed overall in experimental red livery at Camden depot in February 1959.**
T. B. Owen/Colour-Rail BRM469

Above:
Rebuilt 'Patriot' 4-6-0 No 45532 *Illustrious* heads a down express near Lancaster in 1962.
A. E. R. Cope/Colour-Rail BRM171

Below:
Thankfully, black exhausts such as is emitting here from 'Patriot' 4-6-0 No 45519 *Lady Godiva* were rare. The engine is rounding the curve at Dore & Totley in June 1960.
P. J. Hughes/Colour-Rail BRM496

Above:
Gresley three-cylinder 4-6-0 No 61620 *Clumber* of Class B17/6 passes Chaloners Whin with a York-Hull train in May 1957. *W. Oliver/Colour-Rail BRE204*

Below:
The LMS 'Jubilee' 4-6-0s were handsome beasts even when paired with the early, narrow Fowler tenders! Birmingham New Street is host to No 45740 *Munster* preparing to leave with an express for Euston in September 1956. *T. J. Edgington/Colour-Rail BRM294*

TWO

MIXED TRAFFIC MEDLEY

More LMS Class 5 4-6-0s were built than any other tender locomotive class in Britain. A simple, basic, medium sized engine with Swindonian boiler proportions and a good steam distribution and exhaust arrangement, the 'Black 5' was used on any and every type of traffic. They worked express passenger trains to Blackpool, heavy freight over Shap, local stopping trains to Bournemouth and Wick, tourist trains to Kyle of Lochalsh and boat trains to Holyhead.

It is not surprising therefore that such a useful general-purpose loocomotive type had, in general layout, been arrived at by the other companies also. The Great Western 'Hall' class and the 'Modified Hall' derivative performed the same range of tasks within the Western Region. The LNER 'B1' was another similarly laid-out design which met the same need in the east of the country, similar in size to the earlier North Eastern Railway 'B16' 4-6-0s. The Southern had its Maunsell 'H15' 4-6-0s as well, though being derived from a much older design they were not in the same class as the other railways' designs as regards performance.

Above the Class 5 power range, the former railways had gone in differing directions in the mixed traffic field. The LNER had its 'V2' 2-6-2s, a large class of big Gresley machines whose performance often approached that expected of his Pacific locomotives. Indeed the 'V2' design formed the basis of some of the 'A2' class, which was ostensibly a mixed traffic type but which mostly kept to passenger trains.

The LMS had no mixed traffic engine bigger than a Class 5, but the Great Western did produce one larger 4-6-0 type, the 'County' class with 6ft 3in wheels, which again spent most of its life in passenger workings. On the other hand, the '47XX' 2-8-0 engines were basically freight machines which performed as required on passenger extras at summer weekends, as did the SR's 'S15' class 4-6-0s. That the Bulleid light Pacifics were officially mixed traffic was not often taken up in real life.

Every railway had 2-6-0s of a 'go anwhere' specification. Indeed the LMS 'Crabs' and the Stanier equivalents were power class 5, and the LNER 'K3' (Gresley) and 'K1' (Thompson) were strong, rugged beasts as well. The Great Western and the Southern had Moguls of a similar size but different in layout: the '43XX' was a small but strong performer, with inside valve gear; the SR used their outside valve geared 'N' and 'U', and the three-cylinder 'N1' and 'U1' 2-6-0s universally around the Region on all types of traffic up to but not including express trains (if one excludes the Lymington boat trains from that description!). A near match for the '43XX' was the GW 'Manor' class 4-6-0, and slightly larger was the 'Grange' design. With these three types and the 'Hall' 4-6-0, the GW had a strangely close-stepped range of engines, a closeness followed later, surprisingly, among BR's Standard designs. The LNER 'K2' and 'K4' 2-6-0s were ubiquitous in the west of Scotland, the LMS had its modern Ivatt Class 4 2-6-0s and the Southern retained the small class of LB&SCR 'K' 2-6-0s.

When one comes to survey mixed traffic designs of power classes 3 and 2, one finds a virtual dearth of small tender engines specially built for mixed traffic duties. True enough, older freight and passenger locomotives, particularly pre-Grouping ones, often performed mixed traffic turns on branch lines, but to the author's recall only the LMS actually built a new design of small mixed traffic tender locomotive, the Ivatt Class 2 2-6-0. This was intended to enable old branch line engines such as Kirtley 2-4-0s and LNW 'Cauliflowers' to be replaced; which was a laudable objective. Whether it was economic to sink scarce capital into engines destined to work low-traffic and thus by inference uneconomic routes, can be questioned with hindsight. One can assume that the state of the oldest engines at that time rendered such a course inevitable, there being no dieselisation policy north of the GWR.

Which was the most successful mixed traffic class of engine inherited by BR? This is an exceptionally difficult question to answer. In terms of performance, the 'V2' was in a class of its own. However, to compare a 'Black 5' with a 'B1' and a 'Hall' is to talk in shades of grey. No doubt the running of the 'Halls' and Class 5s on the Chester-Birkenhead joint line gave rise to comparisons. Any differences were more likely to be due to the Stephenson and Walschaerts valve gear characteristics than to overall engine and boiler dimensions. Enginemen in Scotland who drove both Class 5s and 'B1s' often said they liked the liveliness of the 'B1s' acceleration on passenger trains, but preferred the 'Black 5s' for hard slogging. The closeness of the merits of these 4-6-0s appears to have led to an interesting compromise in the design of the BR Standard 4-6-0s, which is developed in the appropriate chapter.

Comparison of 2-6-0s in the power class 4 range having a wide field of operation leads us to look at the GWR '43XX', the LMS Ivatt Class 4 2-6-0, the Southern 'N' and 'U' family, and the LNER 'K2' and 'K4' types. All these, other than the Ivatt engines, were based on pre-1923 designs. The 'N' and 'U' were possibly the most modern in concept of these older designs. Construction of an additional number of 'N' class 2-6-0s had been chosen as a post-World War 1 national project at Woolwich Arsenal to relieve unemployment. They were two-cylinder simples with large piston valves and Swindon-style taper boilers. Very strong for their size in terms of their ability to move quite heavy loads briskly, they were slightly under-boilered as a compromise to achieve wider route availability. Examples from the Woolwich build had found their

way to Ireland and Egypt and to the Metropolitan Railway (as 2-6-4Ts), as well as to augment the Southern Railway's own fleet.

However, it was natural that the LMS Ivatt design, being a very free steaming, reliable, lively performer with expectation of long intervals between maintenance and shopping, was regarded by many as the star type in this power range. Some did suggest that its 5ft 3in wheels tended to cause it to become mechanically worn prematurely. Many would thus have liked to have seen a 5ft 8in tender version of the successful Stanier and Fairburn 2-6-4T instead, but this opportunity was not taken up.

The smaller engines were not subjected to the moderate rigours of the 1948 locomotive exchanges programme. In the light of the foregoing discussion, however, BR's choice for future construction proved to be predictable.

Mixed traffic engines were ideal for secondary routes such as in the Scottish highlands. LNER Class K1/1 2-6-0 No 61997 *MacCailin Mor* brings a down freight train along the West Highland line near Glenfinnan.
D. M. C. Hepburne-Scott/Colour-Rail SC401

Left:

The LNER's Class B1 4-6-0 was one of the simplest designs of mixed traffic engine. With the cathedral in the background, No 61160 approaches Lincoln Central in 1960.
Colin Boocock

Left:

A handsome variant of the Stanier Class 5 theme was his 2-6-0 design, of which No 42957 was a smart example when photographed at Horwich in September 1961.
J. G. Dewing/Colour-Rail BRM50

Below:

The GWR possessed four types of mixed traffic 4-6-0 of which the 'Manor' class was the lightest. In this view of the down 'Cambrian Coast Express' passing Pontdolgoch in September 1962, the engine was No 7823 *Hook Norton Manor*. *J. G. Dewing/Colour-Rail BRW16*

The early 'B1's were named, mainly after breeds of deer, hence the class's nickname 'Bongos'! No 61018 *Gnu* pauses at Sleights in May 1964 with a pick-up freight for Whitby.
J. M. Boyes/Colour-Rail BRE199

The most useful mixed traffic locomotives on the Southern Region were Maunsell's series of numerous 2-6-0s. One of the rarer three-cylinder varieties, Class U1 No 31898, leaves Southampton Central station with the daily through train from Brighton to Plymouth in September 1957.

B. J. Swain/Colour-Rail BRS414

The Somerset & Dorset climbed the Mendips in both directions, often necessitating double-heading of the heaviest trains. Two former S&D locomotives, '4F' No 44560 and '7F' No 53806 head the empty stock of a pigeon special, including stock of LMS and GWR origins, at Evercreech New in August 1962. *P. Mullett/Colour-Rail SD77*

In this period scene (August 1959) Class K2/2 2-6-0 No 61787 *Loch Quoich* poses at the old Fort William station. 'K2s' and 'K4s' were the mainstay of the West Highland line passenger and freight services for many years. *R. E. Toop/Colour-Rail SC326*

Above:

4-6-0 No 6879 *Overton Grange* is seen at the head of a down freight near Widney Manor in June 1963.
M. Mensing/Colour-Rail BRW441

Left:

The Great Western introduced the 'County' class 4-6-0s after World War 2. No 1010 *County of Caernarvon* is near Harbury with a down express to Birmingham in July 1963.
A. E. R. Cope/Colour-Rail BRW131

Left:

GW 4-6-0 No 5940 *Whitbourne Hall* faces Plymouth as it awaits departure from Newton Abbot.
P. W. Gray/Colour-Rail BRW203

Stanier Class 5 4-6-0 No 45308 was photographed at Manchester Victoria one December evening in 1961.
N. Harrop/Colour-Rail BRM339

THREE

'BIG FOUR' FREIGHT

In the early days of British Railways, freight trains were typically quite heavy but ran at slow speeds. Usually wagons were small and numerous, and most were not fitted with continuous brakes. This necessitated a brake van at the rear of each train so that the guard could apply the handbrake on his van whenever it was necessary to slow down or to control the train on down-grades. This meant that, on the part of the engine driver, handling of goods trains required gentle acceleration and deceleration, with careful application and release of brakes, in order to avoid snatching of couplings and the possibility of buffer locking or even derailment.

Steam locomotives designed specifically for this type of work characteristically had small coupled wheels for high tractive effort and low speed; more wheels for better adhesion and braking; and relatively moderate boiler power because gentle acceleration did not demand great power outputs.

As a result, the biggest 2-8-0 freight locomotives on the three former railways which dealt with heavy freight (GW, LMS and LNE), although classified '8F' and of high tractive effort, carried boilers little bigger than did other engines of power class 5P or 5MT.

In the 1948 exchanges the LMS '8F' was pitted against the LNER 'O1' 2-8-0, the WD 2-8-0 and 2-10-0 designs and the '28XX' from the Western. The latter proved particularly successful, all the more so bearing in mind its 1903 Churchward origins. The purpose of setting up this group of trials was less clear, because the 2-8-0 type was already available in large numbers. The acquisition of over 700 War Department 2-8-0s after World War 2 virtually eliminated the need for any new construction of heavy, slow-speed freight engines.

Another feature of lower speed operation was its relative kindness to mechanical parts. Freight engines accumulated mileage over a much longer time than did passenger or mixed traffic types. Longevity was not therefore unusual. This was demonstrated notably on the North Eastern Region where the pre-Grouping NER 0-8-0s of Classes Q6 and Q7 survived on coal traffic right through to dieselisation without being replaced by more modern types of steam traction. Similarly the former Great Central 2-8-0s (and their LNER successors) on the Eastern Region were to survive into the 1960s hauling the products of the Yorkshire coalfield. The North Eastern 'J27' 0-6-0s,

heavy engines for that wheel arrangement, also lasted through to dieselisation.

The Southern Railway had three main groups of heavy freight traffic. Cross-London transfer freight was largely in the hands of big tank engines, the ex-LSW 4-8-0T and 4-6-2T engines of massive Urie dimensions, supplemented by Maunsell Class W 2-6-4Ts that were to all intents and purposes tank versions of the 'N1' class. Another group covered the trunk haulage of goods to and from the great docks of Southampton and the other south coast ports. There was also coal traffic from the Kent coalfield, and the usual general distribution of goods and fuel around the Region's territory.

The Southampton Docks freights were exclusively in the capable hands of Maunsell 'S15' 4-6-0s, a design which any other Region would have classified as mixed traffic. Many of these freights were fully vacuum braked, and the 5ft 6in wheels of these hard slogging engines suited their purpose well.

For general freight, O. V. S. Bulleid had supplied the SR with his 40 'Q1' class 0-6-0s. These, and the 20 earlier Maunsell 'Qs', were good, reliable machines.

At the top end of the power spectrum were the LMS Beyer-Garratt 2-6-0+0-6-2Ts. These had been built to eliminate double heading of heavy coal trains such as those which ran from Toton in Nottinghamshire to Brent in north London. The Garratts looked enormous to British eyes, and their qualities have recently been well documented. Suffice it to summarise here, that if their makers' recommendations on steam and exhaust distribution arrangements had been adhered to, they might well have been highly successful performers.

Enormity also appeared in the LNER's Garratt, the 2-8-0+0-8-2T which banked coal trains and heavy freight on the Worsborough incline near Mexborough, before the route was electrified as part of the Manchester-Sheffield-Wath scheme. This locomotive was in effect two Gresley 'O2' 2-8-0s fed by one enormous boiler. One regrets that Britain's liking for slow speeds and loose coupled trains had not encouraged development of a fleet of these. The other giant banker of note, of course, was the Midland's 0-10-0 which assisted trains up the 1 in 37 of the Lickey incline.

At the lower end of the scale, all railways had a host of 0-6-0s of various sizes, the typical British local goods engine in fact. Probably there was not a great deal to choose between most of them, but it is sensible to pick out the GWR's Collett '2251' class for special mention. This type was ostensibly the only 'modern' 0-6-0 outside the Southern Region, and was a particularly good design. It was certainly capable of normal goods work, but it also had a surprising turn of speed, aided by unusually excellent riding qualities for an engine of that arrangement. Thus it found itself quite at home on local passenger duties, more so than many other 0-6-0s which were often pressed into passenger service. For example, one recalls the '4Fs' being driven over the Mendip hills on the Somerset & Dorset line local trains neither running very well nor always steaming all that freely — and producing some extremely metallic noises from their mechanisms!

Other freight engine types which were drafted on to passenger trains were relatively rare, other than on lightly laid branches. The S&DJR '7F' 2-8-0s were excellent machines for taking up to 10 coaches unaided over the Mendips during summer Saturdays, but other 2-8-0s such as 'WDs' and '8Fs', 'O4s' and '28XXs' did not normally deviate from hauling freight traffic. Another exception was the Western's '47XX' 2-8-0 which appeared on holiday extras in the summer months.

Interestingly, BR saw fit not to design any new pure freight engines at all, other than to fill the yawning gap at the top end of the power range. Fast fitted freights up to the year 1950 or so required either mixed traffic engines such as LMS Class 5s, or even bigger machines like the LNER Pacifics and 'V2s'. Six-coupled engines were a serious limitation to the loads which could be started. BR's answer to this need was to be one of the most successful types ever designed for a British railway.

The 'WD' 2-8-0s were the most numerous freight engines on British Railways. No 90243 heads a train of limestone hoppers near Dent in June 1966.
A. E. R. Cope/Colour-Rail BRM548

Above:

The Great Central Railway's Robinson 2-8-0 freight design was selected to be a war engine for overseas service in World War 1. A number subsequently survived on the Great Western as Class ROD. The majority, nearly four hundred, lived their lives on their home territory in Yorkshire, Lincolnshire and Nottinghamshire. Class 04/3 No 63782 plugs steadily along the up loop line at Eaton Wood in June 1959. *P. J. Hughes/Colour-Rail BRE308*

Left:

The Midland Railway's unique four-cylinder 0-10-0 'Big Bertha' had a long and noisy life shoving trains up the 1 in 37 Lickey incline. As BR No 58100 it is seen banking a freight near the summit at Blackwell in 1954. *C. Banks collection/Colour-Rail BRM821*

Left:

The North-east coalfield freights were ably handled by ex-North Eastern Railway motive power right through to dieselisation. Class Q7 0-8-0 No 63471 is seen in September 1960 heading a freight away from Tyne Dock. *T. B. Owen/Colour-Rail BRE438*

Not only were the 'WD' 2-10-0s Riddles' most successful overseas war locomotive design, their arrangement of coupled axle side play was adopted for BR's '9F' 2-10-0 to guarantee its route availability. Twenty five 'WD' 2-10-0s were put to work in Scotland after the war, of which No 90773 was pictured at Grangemouth shed in June 1962.
P. Mullett/Colour-Rail SC420

'Grange' 4-6-0 No 6861 *Crynant Grange* enters Birmingham Snow Hill station with an up freight.
T. J. Edgington/Colour-Rail BRW212

Top:
Britain's most modern light 0-6-0 in concept must have been the Collett Class 2251. Amid snow, the exhaust of No 2261 is lit up as it heads a local goods train near Patney.
P. Strong/Colour-Rail BRW103

Above:
No 30496, the first of R. W. Urie's 'S15' class 4-6-0s makes good speed on a Southampton-bound freight at Winchfield in February 1959. *T. B. Owen/Colour-Rail BRS405*

Left:

The starkly simple lines of Bulleid's 'Q1' class 0-6-0s are well illustrated by this view of No 33010 at Hither Green shed in 1963. Their design was aimed at reducing to a minimum the amount of metal and effort required in their construction. *Colin Boocock*

Left:

The Midland Railway's small engine policy bequeathed to the LMS nothing larger than the '4F' 0-6-0 for freight, although the LMS went on to build many more of them! No 43935 approaches Miller's Dale station with a stopping train from Derby to Manchester Central in 1963. *Colin Boocock*

Below:

A pair of ex-Caledonian 0-6-0s pulls away from Annbank in the Ayrshire coalfield. These engines were typical examples of the most common type of goods locomotive in Britain. Virtually all pre-Grouping railways possessed medium weight 0-6-0s such as these. *Derek Cross/Colour-Rail SC58*

Above:
So useful were the ex-LNWR Class G1 0-8-0s that rebuilding of them to Class G2a with higher boiler pressure continued well into the BR period. No 49350 is pictured on Western Region territory at Oxford shed.
Don Beecroft/Colour-Rail BRW724

Below:
There were over 600 of Stanier's highly successful '8F' class 2-8-0 design. Two, Nos 48352 and 48471, double-head a civil engineers' train at Low Gill.
J. Davenport/Colour-Rail BRM829

FOUR

SMALLER FRY

One of the results of continuous steam locomotive development over 140 years was the production of bigger and bigger engines, culminating in the express passenger machines described in an earlier chapter. As each new top link design appeared, so were earlier express passenger engines relegated to lower links. The express locomotives of the 1920s were by 1948 handling secondary main line work, and the survivors of those built between 1890 and 1920 were distinctly non-express in their daily employment!

The Great Eastern '1500s' (Class B12), Highland 'Castles', GN and LB&SC Atlantics, LSW 'Paddleboxes', LNW 'Prince of Wales' and 'Claughtons' were typically on stopping train duties. Midland 'Compounds', Drummond 'T9s', GE 'Claud Hamiltons', indeed the whole group of middle sized 4-4-0s, found themselves on lighter, local or cross-country line services. The LMS '2Ps' provided power to assist 'Jubilees' on St Pancras-Manchester expresses; so propelled, they reached 90mph on occasions, but their other duties were far more menial.

Since virtually every pre-1923 railway had taken part in this development of express power, there had emerged a plethora of different, if conceptually similar, designs based on the 4-4-0 layout. The norm was two inside cylinders, inside valve gear, and driving wheels of 6ft 6in to 7ft 0in diameter. Early engines were saturated, later ones had superheaters, and many in between were rebuilt from one to the other.

The 4-4-0 type was of such balanced proportions as to encourage the application of engineering artistic flare. Many designs emerged which were beautiful to behold, particularly when resplendent in their early liveries. Take, for example, the Midland and LMS 'Compounds', the Great Eastern 'Clauds', the SE&CR 'D' class, the Great North of Scotland 'D40' breed, and the North Eastern 'D20s'. The GW 'Cities' had disappeared by 1948, but there was still elegance to be seen in diverse corners of the system in the form of a few LNW 4-4-0s, the Billinton 'B4X' class, Drummond's 'T9', and the Caledonian 4-4-0s of McIntosh's design.

Of the later 4-6-0s, downgraded to secondary main line work, was any more handsome than the Southern's 'N15X' 'Remembrance' class? Students of the Great Central and North Eastern 4-6-0s would probably answer, 'Yes!'

This splendid and varied collection of classes presented to British Railways just part of a larger nightmare. Variety of equipment to perform similar tasks carries cost penalties. Spares are multiplied, flexibility in operating is reduced, and knowledge of repair methods is often localised in situations such as this. This variety was repeated in other groups of locomotives: freight engines, passenger tanks, shunting tanks and special types all entered BR's stock lists in their multitudes. There were over 400 different classes of steam locomotives in the newly nationalised British Railways; only some of which can be illustrated here. It is small wonder that BR decided to embark on a programme of construction of new standard classes right down to power groups 4, 3 and 2 in an attempt to bring some order out of the chaos which had been bequeathed by history.

The 0-6-0 wheel arrangement had been popular for freight tender engines for over 100 years. These came in many sizes, small-wheeled for heavy goods, and some with wheels as large as 5ft 3in for faster freight. When Reginald Gardiner, in his classic 'Record of Trains' (prewar 78rpm!) said, 'There comes a time in the life of an engine when it becomes long-funnelled and tiresome', surely he had some of these in mind! Would not the Midland '2F' 0-6-0 fit this description?

The LNW 'Cauliflower', Great Eastern 'J15', LSW '0395' class or Caledonian 'Jumbo' were all examples of elderly, long-chimneyed machines which eked out steady existences up rural lines or on minor colliery branches. Most were at the end of their economic life spans, and BR was faced with the dilemma of how to replace them.

Tank engines also exhibited a huge variety in shapes, sizes, wheel arrangements, ages and purposes. Compare the solid girth of a North Eastern 4-8-0T with a puny Midland 0-4-0ST; the elderly grace of a Great Central or North Eastern 4-6-2T with the modern 2-6-4T replacement (LMS or LNER); the 'J94', '57XX', 'USA' dock tank and LMS 'Jinty', all designed for the same shunting arena and all so different! These were eventually replaced by three BR steam designs, plus a surprising variety of diesel shunter types which is a subject in itself!

Probably the best tank engine designs inherited by BR were the latest LMS types, the Fairburn 2-6-4T and the small Class 2 2-6-2T. The 2-6-4Ts came from a long line of steadily developed engines based on the successful Fowler 2-6-4T, improved with Stanier's taper boiler and the modern features of the Fairburn design itself. H. G. Ivatt's 2-6-2T was a very strong little engine with scope for development into quite a potent machine for its size.

The LNER's latest tank engine design, the 'L1' 2-6-4T from Thompson, proved to be technically inferior, achieving low mileages between overhauls. The Great Western 2-6-2Ts were excellent performers but had not been designed for modern conditions with ease of maintenance in mind. Outside valve gear was preferred in the postwar years.

The Southern had few modern tank engines, other than Maunsell's three-cylinder 'Z' class 0-8-0T and 'W' class 2-6-4T freight engines which were 1920s in concept. The acquired 'USA' 0-6-0Ts were modern, simple and indeed excellent for their purpose. They were among the most modern shunting tanks on BR, sharing this distinction with the Hawksworth '15XX' class outside-cylinder pannier tanks on the Western Region. By the end of the 1940s, however, diesel traction had established itself as the means for providing reliable, single-manned shunting power, and further development of steam for this purpose ceased. The Southern's need for modern passenger tank engines arose from that railway's prewar concentration of investment in electrification, which was followed by World War 2 and the consequential lack of investment in locomotives for secondary activities. This led to two very different solutions being evolved and successively delivered early in the days of BR, as discussed in the next chapter.

Above:
British Railways inherited a multitude of 4-4-0 passenger classes. Among the best were the Southern Maunsell rebuilds of SECR Classes D and E, and his later 'L1' class. One of the latter, No 31789, stands at Ashford in September 1956. *J. M. Jarvis/Colour-Rail BRS223*

Right:
A few early Great Northern 4-4-0s came into BR stock including Class D3 No 2000 (later 62000). Photographed at Grantham just after Nationalisation, it carries decorative green livery specially for its former duties of hauling the LNER directors' saloon. *J. M. Jarvis/Colour-Rail NE36*

Above:
Fowler produced some of the LMS Class 3 2-6-2Ts with condensing apparatus in an attempt to reduce exhaust emissions in long tunnel sections such as the London Metropolitan 'widened lines'. No 40024 was pictured at Moorgate between duties in 1959, with early LT stock as a background. *J. G. Dewing/Colour-Rail BRM61*

Below:
No locomotive type has ever run in Britain in larger numbers than the Great Western's Class 57XX 0-6-0 pannier tanks. Recently overhauled at Newton Abbot works, No 5796 had stopped at the top of Torre bank in April 1957 for wagon brakes to be pinned down on the Kingswear goods. *P. W. Gray/Colour-Rail BRW285*

Above:

The last 2-4-0s in service in Britain were the former Great Eastern 'E4' class. In May 1958 No 62785 pauses at Mildenhall on a branch passenger train.
J. G. Dewing/Colour-Rail BRE20

Left:

BR's smallest passenger tank engines to survive into the 1960s were the GW '14XX' class 0-4-2Ts. Their duties included branch trains such as this one approaching Fowey in Cornwall. *Colin Boocock*

Left:

The last examples of the London & South Western Railway locomotive fleet to run on BR were the Adams 'O2' class 0-4-4Ts in the Isle of Wight which were displaced by electrification! Neat little engines they were, like No W18 *Ningwood* which is drifting out of Ventnor tunnel in June 1964 while running round its train prior to departure for Ryde Pier Head. *P. Mullett/Colour-Rail BRS314*

Above:

There was no better livery (was there?) for a steam locomotive than clean, shiny black, fully lined out in red and grey! Regrettably, black is the most difficult of all to keep looking clean. Stroudley ex-LBSCR Class A1X 0-6-0T No 32677 looks beautiful at Ashford shed in October 1952, repainted and overhauled after its stint of operating push-pull trains on the Isle of Wight. *T. B. Owen/Colour-Rail BRS338*

Left:

The smallest shunting tanks were 0-4-0s used in docks and other locations where track curves were very sharp. The engine at Bridgwater docks in December 1959 was ex-Cardiff Railway 0-4-0ST No 1338 of 1898 vintage. No 1338 was kept especially for this duty, finally being withdrawn in 1963. *J. R. Besley/Colour-Rail BRW511*

Left:

After World War 2, the Southern Railway bought 14 0-6-0Ts, plus one for spares, from the United States Army. These excellent, though simple machines were probably the most modern shunting tank engines in Britain until the introduction in 1949 of Hawksworth's WR '15XX' class 0-6-0PTs. USA 0-6-0T No DS236 is seen in Southern carriage green in 1962, newly delivered after conversion to left hand drive for its spell as Lancing carriage works shunter. *Colin Boocock*

Above:
Class 15XX 0-6-0PT No 1508 was photographed at Cardiff Canton in 1961. *P. J. Hughes/Colour-Rail BRW555*

Left:
Welsh valley coal trains ran short distances but needed high tractive effort locomotives. The GWR provided two classes of 2-8-0T and 2-8-2T which were ideal for the task. '5205' class 2-8-0T No 5264 heads a coal train away from Aberbeeg in October 1962. *W. Potter/Colour-Rail BRW275*

Left:
Some old engines survived their contemporaries in departmental service. One of the LNWR's so-called 'Special Tanks', 0-6-0ST *Earlestown*, is seen shunting at Wolverton carriage works in the 1950s. *Colour-Rail BRM391*

Top:
One or two engines outlived their peers for decades because their special route availability suited particular locations.
The Wenford Bridge branch in Cornwall was one of these, and was host to the three Beattie ex-LSWR 2-4-0 well tanks dating from 1874. No 30587 was pictured in Pencarrow Woods in April 1961, aged 87!
D. M. C. Hepburne-Scott/Colour-Rail BRS498

Above:
Adams 'O2' class 0-4-4T No 30200 is seen with the 4.40pm Padstow-Bodmin North service near Grogley Halt in September 1960. *P. W. Gray/Colour Rail BRS252*

In the bleak countryside of the Scottish highlands, ex-Caledonian Railway 0-4-4T No 55217 waits with the branch train at Killin in May 1959.
W. J. V. Anderson/Colour-Rail SC133

FIVE

MORE OF THE SAME

While the policy for building standard BR steam locomotive designs was being developed, the need existed in the years from 1948 to 1951 for construction of new locomotives to existing Regional designs.

The London Midland Region went on turning out 'Black 5s' in considerable numbers, including developments with roller bearing axleboxes and manganese steel axlebox and horn liners. Construction also continued of the Ivatt Class 4 2-6-0, his two Class 2 designs (2-6-0 and 2-6-2T) and the Fairburn 2-6-4T.

This new building enabled many of the remaining pre-Grouping designs to be eliminated. The LNWR 'Claughton' and 'Prince of Wales' 4-6-0s at length disappeared, and the last Hughes L&YR 4-6-0 No 50455 was scrapped. The individualistic Scottish companies' few remaining 4-6-0s were quickly eliminated. L&YR 0-8-0s also disappeared and the Midland '3P' 4-4-0s died away. By far the most thorough slaughter however, was the almost total elimination of things LNW: the 'Cauliflowers', 'Coal Tanks' and 'Special Tanks' became memories, and great inroads were made into the ranks of 'G2' 0-8-0s. These engines suffered from light frame construction and were consequently becoming expensive to maintain.

On the Western Region more new 'Castles' appeared, as did further 'Modified Halls', and (more surprisingly, in view of the success of diesel shunters) batches of '94XX' class pannier tanks were constructed, some of which were to see very few years of service indeed.

The WR new construction led quickly to the elimination of many favourite types such as the 'Star' and 'Saint' 4-6-0s, the 'Bulldog' 4-4-0s and 'Dean Goods' 0-6-0s. Odd special classes such as the Midland & South Western Junction 2-4-0s and many South Wales railways' remnants (mainly 0-6-2Ts) disappeared in the early BR years together with the Cambrian 0-6-0s and the last of the GW 0-6-0PTs with open-backed cabs. The Robinson ROD 2-8-0s did not last long into BR, but in this case their demise was in the wake of the arrival of the 'WD' 2-8-0s.

The Eastern and North Eastern Regions continued to turn out 'B1s', 'K1s', 'L1s' and 'A2' Pacifics (the Peppercorn variety). The 'A1' class actually began to emerge in 1948. The most surprising new build on the whole of BR was the decision to turn out from Darlington works a new batch of the North Eastern Railway design 0-6-0T of Class J72. Being a pre-Grouping design, these were thought of as old-fashioned by all who saw them. The need for shunting locomotives in the North-east must have been exceptionally urgent!

New 'B1s' and 'K1s' in their profusion made inroads into pre-Grouping passenger designs on the Eastern and North Eastern systems. All the remaining Great Central 4-6-0s and most of the popular 'Director' 4-4-0s took their leave; Scotland lost its North British 'Scott' class 4-4-0s. The last Great Northern 4-4-0s went, as did most GE 'B12' and 'D16' passenger engines. Smaller machines such as the GE 2-4-0s and 2-4-2Ts did not survive very long into BR, either.

The Southern Region produced the third batch of 'Merchant Navy' class 4-6-2s as well as many light Pacifics during the early BR years. However, the SR's need for new passenger tank engines to replace ancient varieties such as the 'M7' and 'H' 0-4-4Ts and the I1X and I3 4-4-2Ts had not been met. O. V. S. Bulleid had quoted this need in proposing his new general purpose bogie locomotive, the 'Leader' class, the first of which began trials in 1949. Strenuous efforts were made to resolve technical shortcomings but it became clear that the 'Leader' would not be successful. The trials were quickly terminated, and No 36001 and its four partly-completed sisters were scrapped. The BR corporate solution to the SR's tank engine problem was the simple expedient of supplying the Region with the most suitable existing types available elsewhere: the LMS Class 4 2-6-4T and Class 2 2-6-2T. The 2-6-4Ts were built in Brighton works, and settled down well on the Central and Eastern Sections, while the 2-6-2Ts began to make inroads into the 'O2s' and 'M7s'.

The large numbers of new Bulleid 4-6-2s enabled older classes such as most of the Drummond 4-4-0s (other than the 'T9s') and the LBSC 'B4Xs' to be eliminated by displacement, together with 'H1' Atlantics and 'Remembrance' and 'T14' 4-6-0s. Many early 0-6-0 classes were also withdrawn.

The 'LMS engine' solution was also applied to certain areas of the former LNER. Fairburn tanks took over, for example, the Rickmansworth-Aylesbury services. Ivatt Class 4 2-6-0s became common on the M&GN lines, and Class 2 2-6-0s braved the wilds of the Pennines on the routes across from the North-east. The Class 2s even found their way on to the Western Region to displace 'Dean Goods' 0-6-0s. At this point some shortcomings emerged within the 2-6-0s. There was clearly a need to improve this modern breed. A later chapter outlines the excellent improvements BR made to several of the former railways' types, in the interests of more effective and efficient operation.

Mention should perhaps be made at this juncture of the spread of the 733 'WD' 2-8-0s across BR, and of the 25 'WD' 2-10-0s sent to the Scottish Region. Only the Southern needed no 'WDs'. All other Regions found these extremely simple engines competent handlers of freight. The plain looks and ability to run with low maintenance made them appear unlovely and unloved. Their survival to the end of steam on BR was a testimony to their abilities. They were sprightly and strong freight haulage machines capable of matching the performance of the Regional 2-8-0 types. Their high route availability and ease of maintenance made them universally acceptable. In many ways the Riddles 'WD' 2-8-0 might be considered to have been given the role of BR's first Standard design.

Regional Classes built for British Railways
Eastern and North Eastern Regions:
  'A1' 4-6-2*
  'A2/3' 4-6-2
  'B1' 4-6-0
  'K1' 2-6-0*
  'L1' 2-6-4T
  'J72' 0-6-0T

London Midland Region:
  8P 4-6-2
  5 4-6-0
  4 2-6-4T Fairburn
  4 2-6-0 Ivatt
  2 2-6-0 Ivatt
  2 2-6-2T Ivatt

Southern Region:
  'Merchant Navy' 4-6-2
  'West Country' 4-6-2†
  'Leader' 0-6-6-0T*

Western Region:
  'Castle' 4-6-0
  'Modified Hall' 4-6-0
  'Manor' 4-6-0
  15XX 0-6-0PT*
  16XX 0-6-0PT*
  51XX 2-6-2T
  57XX 0-6-0PT
  74XX 0-6-0PT
  94XX 0-6-0PT

† Includes 'Battle of Britain' class.
* Class introduced after Nationalisation.

NB: Rebuilding continued of 'Royal Scot' 4-6-0s with taper boilers, and of ex-LNWR 'G1' 0-8-0s into 'G2A' class, after Nationalisation.

Left:
The Peppercorn 'A1' class three-cylinder 4-6-2 design emerged in 1949 to swell the East Coast main line fleet. In January 1962 No 60152 *Holyrood* **leaves St Boswells on a Waverley route train for Carlisle.**
D. M. C. Hepburne-Scott/ Colour-Rail SC364

Above:
The ex-LMS 'Black 5' design was multiplied in the early years of British Railways. One of the BR-built engines, No 44999, leaves Aberdeen with a southbound fish train in 1962. *D. R. Bissett/Colour-Rail SC356*

Below:
'Castles' continued to emerge from Swindon Works at least until 1950. In June 1962 No 7031 *Cromwell's Castle* leaves Paddington with the 4.45pm to Wolverhampton. *P. W. Gray/Colour-Rail BRW411*

Top:
Apart from one solitary prototype, all the ER/NER Class K1 2-3-0s were built in BR days. Alnwick is the setting for a June 1966 departure by No 62011.
E. Wilson/Colour-Rail BRE416

Above:
The Fairburn 2-6-4Ts, such as No 42138 seen here running round its train at Oxenhope in 1956, were built in large numbers by BR, some even at Brighton Works for the Southern Region. *T. J. Edgington/Colour-Rail BRM307*

Top:
The last 10 Bulleid 'Merchant Navy' Pacifics, plus many of the light Pacifics, entered service in 1948/49. No 35024 *East Asiatic Company* **looks superb in the early BR blue livery when heading a down Weymouth train at Waterloo in June 1949.** *S. C. Townroe/Colour-Rail BRS307*

Above:
BR also built new 'Modified Hall' 4-6-0s. '6959' class 4-6-0 No 7924 *Thornycroft Hall* **passes Twyford with an up express in the winter of 1959.**
T. B. Owen/Colour-Rail BRW610

Below:

Another GWR design of which further examples were built by British Railways was the 'Manor' class. One of these, No 7822 *Foxcote Manor* is seen near Llanbadarn with the morning train to Shrewsbury in December 1958.
T. B. Owen/Colour-Rail BRW448

Bottom:

Some LMS Ivatt Class 2 2-6-0s were built for Western Region routes. One of these, No 46506, is seen with a Moat Lane-Brecon local train near Llanidloes in April 1954.
T. B. Owen/Colour-Rail BRW524

Above:

Painters put the finishing touches to the first Bulleid 'Leader' class 0-6-6-0T No 36001 in Eastleigh Works yard in June 1949. Considerable effort was made to pursue the tests of this engine, but its design problems were not overcome, and the class was prematurely scrapped.
S. C. Townroe/Colour-Rail BRS331

Left:

The North Eastern Railway 0-6-0T design of Class J72 dating from 1898, would hardly seem to be a suitable type of which to build new examples as late as the 1950s, but a batch was constructed by British Railways at Darlington. One of these, No 69008, is seen beneath the gantry at Tyne Dock shed exit in 1951. *J. Robertson/Colour-rail BRE 414*

Left:

Unliked by enthusiasts who called them 'Doodlebugs' or 'Pigs', the Ivatt Class 4 2-6-0s were in fact very competent engines in their single chimney form. One of the BR-built examples, No 43157, skirts the coast near Caister on Sea in April 1957 with the 3.51pm Yarmouth Beach-Melton Constable on the former MGNJR.
E. Alger/Colour-Rail BRE605

SIX

NEW STANDARDS

If a standard range of new steam locomotives was to be produced for BR, several key decisions were doubtless required to be made quickly:

How many different designs were needed to encompass the range of duties?
Should the best existing Regional designs be repeated?
What level of steam technology should be embodied?
To what extent should common components be employed?
How could the new designs balance simplicity with efficiency?
What were the priorities for construction?

The Railway Executive member for mechanical and electrical engineering, R. A. Riddles, had appointed his senior engineers principally from former LMS men. While the aim was to utilise the best practices available, it is not surprising that the LMS influence could be detected throughout the BR Standard locomotive range. Features such as tapered boilers with Belpaire fireboxes, dished smokebox doors, rocking and drop grates, manganese steel axlebox and horn liners, long travel piston valves driven by outside Walschaerts gear, high temperature superheat, high running plates for clear access to moving parts for maintenance and narrowed tender coal spaces for improved backwards view all came from the latest LMS practice.

However, Riddles' desire for the engines to stand out as of BR rather than Regional origin was dealt with by the adoption of a dominant, new exterior design style. This picked out certain common details such as deep valances, enclosed cab layout (new design), chimney tops (actually pure L&YR in shape!), smokebox fronts (GW and Stanier LMS) and smoke deflectors (LNER), to give a family likeness to all engines in the range. The only notable deviations occurred with the smaller locomotives: the Brighton-designed 2-6-4T had curved sides to the tank, cab and bunker, and the Class 3 2-6-2T and both Class 2 types avoided the deep valances to the running plates.

The first engine to appear was the Class 7 Pacific No 70000 *Britannia*. This was a completely new design which bore no direct relationship to any Regional type. The boiler, in size close to a Bulleid 'West Country', had a wide copper firebox. The 6ft 2in coupled wheels could have been either Bulleid or Thompson inspired. The two-cylinder layout was unique among British Pacific classes. At the time (1951) it was announced that this had been made possible by advances in balancing theory since the former railways' 4-6-2s had been designed. In fact, the Germans had operated bigger two-cylinder 4-6-2s in express services since 1925.

Observers were surprised that only a single blast pipe and chimney were provided on No 70000. In reality, this produced sufficient draught for an engine designed to be worked with full regulator and not-too-short cut-off settings. Drivers coped with this feature with different results. There was no problem on the GE lines where hard-pressing of locomotives was not unusual; on the WR many could not come to terms with the different handling required. Generally, the 'Britannias' could perform brilliantly and economically, and fully justified their batch production straight off the drawing board. Crews appreciated the enclosed cabs and well-placed controls, though SR drivers regretted the absence of electric lighting. The GE batch revolutionised train speeds on the Norwich and Cambridge main lines.

More controversy surrounded the Class 6 'Clan' 4-6-2 when that appeared. Basically a 'Britannia' with a smaller boiler, its introduction was presumably to meet a need for power on lines of lower route availability. They were deployed on the Glasgow & South Western routes and on the northern end of the West Coast main line. No more than 10 were built and hindsight indicates they found no unique role to fill.

The Class 5 4-6-0, on the other hand, had the potential to be built in large numbers. Its boiler was clearly based on the LMS Class 5. The engine used the same 6ft 2in wheels as did the Standard Pacifics, and its valve gear, also like the 4-6-2s, was clearly Doncaster inspired. The result was an excellent machine, capable of being flogged without steaming difficulties, and able to run fast when required. It was also at home on fitted freight work. The Standard 5's performance edge over the LMS 'Black 5', the 'B1' and 'Hall' was not so significant as to dampen Regional preferences for their own designs, except on the Southern where they beat the 'King Arthurs' on their own ground, and on the Somerset & Dorset where they remained the firm favourites from their introduction to the closure of

61

that line. A group of engines was also supplied with Caprotti valve gear, towards the end of the class deliveries. Operationally, the Standard Class 5s worked predominantly on the Scottish, Southern and London Midland Regions.

Next down the scale came the three Class 4 designs. No 80010 was the first 2-6-4T to be delivered. Essentially a tidied-up Fairburn 2-6-4T, these machines were built in relatively large numbers for all Regions except the Western (whose Prairie tanks ruled the roost until dieselisation). The Class 4 4-6-0 was a strange beast, virtually a Class 5 with smaller boiler, cylinders and 5ft 8in wheels. It was in the operating range of the WR 'Manor' 4-6-0 but had no other real Regional equivalent. The Class 4 4-6-0s went principally to the Western, London Midland and Southern Regions. They worked capably but rarely exceptionally. There was also the Class 4 2-6-0, clearly based on the Ivatt Class 4 2-6-0 in all principal dimensions but with a big improvement in looks. These worked very well indeed on Southern, Eastern, North Eastern and LM Region secondary services, though they tended to become mechanically quite rough at high mileages.

One can with hindsight regret that the obvious derivative was not built. A 2-6-0 version of the 5ft 8in 2-6-4T would have been a winner in performance and general flexibility, as versatile as the former NCC 2-6-0 type in Northern Ireland. It might have equalled the 4-6-0's performance, bettered the 5ft 3in 2-6-0, and reduced the variety of boiler designs by one, had it been substituted for the other two designs.

The Class 3 2-6-0 was a Class 4 2-6-0 with a smaller boiler, not as small as the Ivatt Class 2 boiler, but reportedly based on that of a GW Prairie. This was another class not built in large numbers. One wonders in retrospect whether the gap between the Class 4 and Class 2 was really worth bridging. It had a 2-6-2T derivative, used quite widely on SR and WR branches, but they were occasionally quite competently deputised for by Class 2s. The Class 3 2-6-2T was a handsome tank engine, certainly, and sufficiently liked on the Western to receive green livery in later years.

The smallest standard designs were the Class 2 2-6-0 and 2-6-2T, basically Ivatt engines without top feeds and with minor detail differences only. Indeed, most parts were common with the LMS engines, even though their drawing numbers were changed to BR ones, thus disguising their LMS origins! Both classes were good performers. The 2-6-2Ts were fitted with vacuum push-pull control apparatus. In this form a few were transferred to replace push-pull fitted 'M7s', only to find that the SR push-pull system used compressed air to operate the regulator remotely! The push-pull gear was removed by the SR at Eastleigh works.

Then came the '9Fs'. These 2-10-0s were the only BR Standard design that met an operating need that could not have been covered by a Regional type. Col H. C. B. Rogers' book *Riddles and the '9Fs'* (Ian Allan) describes their design and history succinctly. They were clearly quite excellent engines. The boiler was slightly smaller than the Class 7, redesigned so as to pitch the wide firebox over 5ft 0in coupled wheels, a feat never previously achieved within the British loading gauge. The 10-coupled wheelbase embodied the curving flexibility which Riddles had used on his 'WD' 2-10-0s, and the use of minimal rotating balancing produced an engine capable of a surprising turn of speed.

The '9Fs' were ideal for the heavy, fitted freight regime which was spreading across British Railways. They handled block oil trains with as much ease as heavy coal trains, and came, almost too late, to be the only locomotive able to take 12-coach passenger trains over the Mendips without a pilot locomotive. Indeed, the fact that they could run at up to 90mph with 5ft 0in, 10-coupled wheels put them onto main line expresses on occasions as deputies for Pacifics!

Ten '9Fs' were built with Crosti feed water heating drums under a slightly smaller boiler design than the standard '9Fs'. The aim was to achieve an efficiency improvement to match that claimed for Italian locomotives so fitted. It is, however, always difficult to improve on the excellent. While thermal efficiency did improve, increased maintenance costs were caused by corrosion in the preheater drums. The drums were subsequently removed and the locomotives converted to a normal layout. They retained their smaller boilers, however, and their odd looks.

The '9F' 2-10-0 No 92220 *Evening Star* was BR's last new steam locomotive, but the '9F' class was not the last new steam class to be introduced to BR. While other types were under construction, No 71000 *Duke of Gloucester* emerged as the prototype Class 8P 4-6-2. Not as large as an LMS or LNER 8P Pacific, No 71000's development period was brief and the design was not put into series production. It used a Class 7 boiler barrel with a longer firebox, over a three-cylinder layout using Caprotti poppet valve gear for effective steam distribution. Why its maximum theoretical output was not achieved may yet be revealed, operating in preservation, following modifications to the ashpan and draughting.

We are now blessed with hindsight, through which we can form views on the variety of Standard classes actually produced. Clearly, the close spacing of 11 of the 12 designs enabled any engine to deputise for one in the next higher power class. Such operating flexibility was used, certainly. But the principle was not followed on the Southern, and not always either on overseas systems. An alternative would be to build fewer types at wider power spacings, ensuring that sufficient number were built at the 'big engine' end of the spectrum. Had this policy been adopted, the BR designs could have been reduced to the number of classes shown in the accompanying table, assuming the appearance of a 2-6-0 tender version of the 2-6-4T.

There could then have been eight instead of 12 locomotive types, and six instead of 10 boiler designs.

BR Standard Steam Classes — an Alternative Range

Power Class	Type	Wheel diameter	Boiler size
'9F'	2-10-0	5ft 0in	9F
'8P'	4-6-2	6ft 2in	8P
'7MT'	4-6-2	6ft 2in	7
'5MT'	4-6-0	6ft 2in	5
'4MT'	2-6-0	5ft 8in	4
'4MT'	2-6-4T	5ft 8in	4
'2MT'	2-6-0	5ft 0in	2
'2MT'	2-6-2T	5ft 0in	2

A list of classes actually built is near the end of Appendix 1.

It is probably churlish to make such suggestions, because the Standard range provided BR with an effective and economical fleet of steam locomotives which could have held the fort competently until the advent of widespread main line electrification. The change in policy towards rapid dieselisation and the rationalisation of the BR system, which together caused the Standard locomotives to have such short lives, were no reflection on the locomotives themselves.

It was an odd quirk of fate, was it not, which resulted in building ceasing when the BR Standard locomotive fleet had reached just one short of its first thousand?

The good looks of the 'Britannias' matched their spritely performance on the Great Eastern main line services. No 70003 *John Bunyan* is portrayed at Thetford in March 1962. *J. J. Davis/Colour-Rail BRE248*

The '9F' 2-10-0 design filled an urgent need for heavy freight power most effectively. No 92064 is pictured at Stanley with coal for Consett. *J. G. Dewing/Colour-Rail BRE609*

The free running '9F' 2-10-0s were ideal for passenger trains on the heavily graded Somerset & Dorset line. The 9.53am from Bath to Bournemouth West passes a trackside garden at Midsomer Norton in August 1962 with No 92001 at the head. *P. Mullett/Colour-Rail SD67*

Above:
Only 10 'Clans' were built and they spent most of their lives on West Coast services north of Preston, and on the Glasgow & South Western lines. In June 1961 No 72003 *Clan Fraser* heads a Liverpool-Glasgow train near Greenholm.
Derek Cross/Colour-Rail BRM325

Below:
One of the competent BR Class 5 4-6-0s, No 73015, climbs the Lickey incline with a northbound passenger working in 1956. *W. A. Thompson/Colour-Rail BRM518*

Top:
Another Standard Class 5 photographed in 1963 brings a freight through Nottingham Victoria station.
Don Beecroft/Colour-Rail BRE603

Above:
The Standard Class 4 2-6-0, represented here by No 76017 photographed after overhaul at Eastleigh, was a neat design and a lively performer. *Colin Boocock*

Left:
The medium size Class 3 2-6-0 was in effect a Class 4 with a smaller boiler. In Scotland in March 1961, No 77015 crosses Glenbuck Loch causeway with a Muirkirk local.
Derek Cross/Colour-Rail SC89

Class 3 2-6-2T No 82020 stands at Machynlleth shed in September 1962, carrying unlined green livery.
J. G. Dewing/Colour-Rail BRW31

On the Western Region's Cambrian line near Carno, Standard Class 2 2-6-0 No 78003 makes a charming picture as it hauls a short school train in September 1962.
J. G. Dewing/Colour-Rail BRW33

Right:
The well-balanced lines of the BR Class 4MT Standard 2-6-4T design are displayed by No 80153, seen at Eastleigh depot in April 1957, just outshopped from an Intermediate overhaul. *Colin Boocock*

Below:
The solitary '8P' Pacific No 71000 *Duke of Gloucester* poses at Camden depot. *J. G. Dewing/Colour-Rail BRM12*

Left:
Class 2 2-6-2T No 84014 crosses Park Bridge on the Oldham Clegg Street line in 1965. *B. Magilton/Colour-Rail BRE520*

SEVEN

IMPROVING THE BREED

The early postwar years were not a time of plenty, as many had supposed they would be. Six years of national economic activity had deen diverted towards defeating Hitler's Naziism on the European continent, and in stemming the tide of Japanese imperialism in the Far East. For many years afterwards the armed forces retained large numbers of manpower. The years of civil and industrial reconstruction which followed the war were marked by various shortages, including manpower and fuel. Such were not ideal conditions for running a fleet of ageing steam locomotives in an era when public expectations were high. In Britain there were intense demands to raise train speeds to prewar levels, yet the 1930s-type availability of good steam coal and relatively cheap manpower were not likely to be repeated.

Consequently, there was a need to improve on many of the older express steam locomotive types which had been designed for more ideal operating conditions than obtained in BR days. Quite a number of the newer designs which had appeared in more recent years also required improvement in the light of early experience.

The coal quality situation affected locomotives designed for specific types of coal. Those of the Great Western Railway, for example, steamed best on good Welsh steam coal. That railway had blessed its vast locomotive works at Swindon with a locomotive testing plant on which engines could be run on rollers linked to dynamometers which could absorb and record the output from the locomotive. This enabled a locomotive to be tested in controlled conditions statically, which in turn facilitated the measurement of performance indicators such as cylinder and exhaust pressures, blast pipe pressure, superheater steam temperatures, and smokebox vacuum. British Railways also commissioned a more modern test plant at Rugby which was able to handle the largest Pacific locomotives. The Rugby plant carried out a number of detailed tests on principal classes, and the published test reports proved valuable in making comparisons as well as enabling potential improvements to be pinpointed.

Both test plants were in the charge of teams of engineers able to analyse test results and to derive from the findings intelligent solutions to problems. In many ways, the Swindon team could probably claim the greater success rate, because most significant and simple solutions to locomotive steaming problems emerged as a result of their work.

Thus it was that, after more than 25 years of operating 'Kings' and 'Castles' with relatively low superheat, these locomotives were brought into line with those of the other Regions and were fitted with high temperature superheat. The experiments with draughting on the Swindon test plant resulted in all the 'Kings' being fitted with double blastpipes and chimneys, which gave their performance on the road a new lease of life, and fortunately did not diminish their stylish appearance. The 'Castles' had always been good performers in their class, and, as was to happen with other classes subsequently, it proved less easy to improve upon a winner. The fitting of double chimneys to 'Castles' (like Bulleid's fitting of Lemaître exhausts to SR 'Schools') was not pursued beyond a relatively small number. On the other hand, the relatively modern 'County' class 4-6-0 did find benefit, and all were fitted with double chimneys, in this case a squat variety that was shorter than the other boiler mountings.

As mentioned in the chapter on new building of Regional types, the LMS Ivatt Class 2 2-6-0 design which had been brought onto Welsh border routes to displace 'Dean Goods' 0-6-0s was being criticised by train crews, so one of the 2-6-0s was put on the Swindon test rollers. It was found that the Derby design had too wide a chimney to enable adequate draughting of the fire for good steam production. Following fitting of a correctly proportioned chimney, the resulting improvement brought the boiler up to an excellent standard of steaming that matched the undoubted strength of the engine. All subsequent builds of this class and its mate, the Class 2 2-6-2T, incorporated the narrow internal chimney dimensions, though the later ones had a double-walled chimney casting which enabled a more aesthetically satisfactory external chimney profile to be achieved.

The other Ivatt 2-6-0 design, his Class 4, had been fitted from new with a double blastpipe and chimney. This engine, in contrast to most others needing modification, was over-draughted in this form; the ability to draw unburned fuel from the fire and throw it out of the chimney does not lead to economy, however well the boiler steams! In this case the solution was a single blastpipe and chimney, which as a compensation also much improved the locomotive's appearance. Nevertheless, these engines laboured under disagreeable nicknames varying from 'Doodlebugs' to 'Pigs' throughout their useful lives.

It was on the LNER big engine fleet that some of the most startling progress was made. Sir Nigel Gresley had already fitted double Kylchap exhausts to some 'A4s' before the war, and *Mallard's* 126mph bore testimony to the free running which that device encouraged. Not only did it raise the draught available for the fire, it also reduced the back-pressure at the blastpipe. Quite logically, therefore, all the 'A4s' received this device, as did all the Thompson and Peppercorn Pacifics from new.

British Railways was able to develop this theme further with the 'V2' 2-6-2s and the old 'A3' class 4-6-2s. On these classes new cylinders were provided, the outward, visible sign being straight, outside steam pipes to the outside cylinders. Double Kylchaps were fitted, and the transformation was almost complete. The 'A3' class performance reached levels in normal traffic that had rarely been surpassed in prewar years, so good was the improvement achieved. One snag was the drifting of steam to obscure the driver's view, resulting from the lower exhaust pressure. Uniquely in British practice, the 'A3s' were fitted with German style 'blinker' smoke deflector plates either side of the smokebox. Controversial though this undoubtedly was in the eyes of the many who loved the classic Great Northern lines of these lovely engines, it did bring to their appearance a modern image which matched their excellent performance!

In the case of the Bulleid Pacifics, there were problems a-many to resolve. The cut-off drift at speed due to the valve gear characteristics has already been mentioned, as have their high maintenance costs and relatively low reliability, though they were becoming more dependable as detail difficulties were systematically resolved by the engineers. The draughting of the boilers and the free running of the engines were never in doubt. Therefore the process of rebuilding these locomotives was begun. The Bulleid valve gear gave way to three independent sets of Walschaerts, curing at a stroke the cut-off and overrun problems. Steam reverse was replaced by an accurate manual screw reverse so that control was secure. The steam control to the firehole door was removed in the interests of simplicity. The plate 'dustbin' chimney and petticoat were replaced by properly shaped castings and a new ashpan was fitted; both were changes which improved the completeness of combustion. Manganese steel axlebox and horn liners were fitted, to extend the period between overhauls. Frame stretchers were strengthened, and the coupled wheels rebalanced. A cylindrical smokebox was riveted flush with the front ring of the boiler barrel. The air-smoothed casing gave way to conventional exterior 'furniture' designed to bring the Pacifics' appearance close to the BR Standard family looks.

The rebuilt Bulleid Pacifics were totally successful. At around £8,500 each the work was expensive. A back check was carried out on savings actually achieved from better coal consumption and lower maintenance and overhaul costs. This proved that the rebuilding work had paid for itself. As for the myth that free running had been impaired by the change in valve gear, top speeds of the rebuilt 'Merchant Navy' locomotives were recorded above 100mph, just as before rebuilding. All 30 'MNs' and 60 of the 110 light Pacifics were rebuilt, before the work ceased in the light of the realisation that steam's life expectancy was now short.

Of the BR Standard designs, only one appeared to need improvement. The Class 4 4-6-0 met most of the needs of its power class, but was lacking in reserve when called upon to deputise for bigger Class 5 locomotives. Some Class 4 4-6-0s were fitted with double chimneys and blastpipes, which rectified this problem, an interesting contrast to what befell the LMS Ivatt Class 4 2-6-0s!

Nevertheless the desire to tinker is always there, and one '9F' was fitted with a Giesl ejector chimney, as was one unrebuilt 'Battle of Britain' Pacific. In neither case did the device produce more than a marginal improvement, illustrating how well the steam circuits and draughting of modern steam engines had been developed. (The Giesl ejector had worked very well on older, less efficient engines overseas.)

One can conclude that BR's steam locomotive policy was broad and positive in outlook. Not only were good, modern standard designs produced, they were backed by intelligently improved older locomotives. Towards the end of steam, there were very few 'duds', if any, in BR's locomotive stud.

Left:

The rebuilding of the Stanier 'Turbomotive' turbine 4-6-2 produced this splendidly handsome engine, reminiscent of a cross between a 'Princess Royal' and a 'Duchess'. No 46202 was unhappily destroyed in the Harrow & Wealdstone accident in 1952. *W. H. Foster/Colour-Rail BRM789*

Below:

Double blastpipes and chimneys together with higher temperature superheat put new life into the ex-GWR 'King' class 4-6-0s. No 6019 *King Henry V* scatters the contents of the water troughs at Goring as it speeds towards Paddington with the up 'Red Dragon' in March 1961. *T. B. Owen/Colour-Rail BRW389*

Above:
The double chimney on 'County' class 4-6-0 No 1007 *County of Brecknock* had a squat appearance. The locomotive was photographed in August 1959 leaving Saltash with the 'Cornish Riviera Limited' T. B. Owen/Colour-Rail BRW602

Left:
A rejuvenated 'A3' 4-6-2 with double Kylchap exhaust, No 60103 *Flying Scotsman*, heads the down 'Yorkshire Pullman' in August 1960 near Hadley Wood.
J. F. Aylard/Colour-Rail BRE90

Left:
The Southern attempted to curb the spark throwing of the Lemaitre five-jet blast pipe by replacing it on No 35019 *French Line CGT* with a single blastpipe and chimney. This 'Merchant Navy' was thus noisier to the ear, and in this form it is seen passing Shawford in the winter of 1954.
B. J. Swain/Colour-Rail BRS376

Above:

Fitting a double chimney and blastpipe to the Standard 4 4-6-0s such as No 75029, seen here in 1966 at Machynlleth, enabled these locomotives to steam better when working at the upper end of their power range.

J. R. Besley/Colour-Rail BRW571

Below:

No 35024 *East Asiatic Company* exhibits the handsome lines of the rebuilt 'Merchant Navy' class as it pauses at Southampton Central.

G. W. Parry collection/Colour-Rail BRS472

Left:

Bulleid Pacifics of both groups were rebuilt to improve their maintenance and fuel costs. The train engine of this Manchester-Bournemouth relief to the down 'Pines Express' is rebuilt 'West Country' No 34040 *Crewkerne*. 4-6-0 No 75027 provides head end assistance for the Mendip inclines. The photograph was taken at Midford on the Somerset & Dorset line in 1962. *W. Potter/Colour-Rail SD142*

Left:

Some Maunsell 'N' and 'U' class 2-6-0s were improved by being given new cylinders and BR Standard design chimneys. 'N' 2-6-0 No 31853 sported these modifications in August 1960 when working a Padstow train near Halwill. *Don Beecroft/Colour Rail BRS474*

Below:

Ugly is as ugly does! The 10 Crosti '9F' 2-10-0s were not an improvement on the standard '9F' design because severe corrosion within the pre-heating barrel caused excessive maintenance costs. No 92028 was seen at Finedon Road in July 1959. *K. C. H. Fairey/Colour-Rail BRM615*

EIGHT

HOMES AND HOSPITALS

Along with its 20,000 steam locomotives, British Railways inherited an infrastructure of about 350 depots to which the locomotives were allocated for maintenance, and 21 locomotive works capable of undertaking periodic overhauls.

It sometimes comes as a surprise to be reminded how much attention steam locomotives required. As an example of the most basic work necessary to keep an old engine running, one can recall that on arrival at Ventnor on the Isle of Wight, after less than 20 miles of a return trip to Ryde Pier Head, it was necessary for the fireman to open the smokebox door and shovel from the smokebox volumes of ash which had collected around the foot of the blastpipe just behind the door. To save time this was done while the 'O2' 0-4-4T took water. Modern types of engine were fitted with deflector plates within the smokebox which were designed to direct the draught to pick up loose deposits and fling them up the chimney. This so-called 'self-cleaning' smokebox was one device designed to reduce the labour content of steam operation.

Basic attention needed at least once every working day included coaling. Whilst locomotive water tanks could be and were replenished at stations, yards or loops en route, filling of bunkers or tenders with coal required a visit to a depot, or at least one of the small sub-depots at strategic locations. Coaling methods varied substantially. Major depots often had high, concrete coaling plants, capable of hopper discharge straight into a tender or bunker. These plants were usually fed by lifting a coal wagon on a hoist up the side of the tower, and tippling it at the top so that its contents fell into the large hopper below. Use of such plants was relatively efficient in labour, but had the disadvantage of preventing special selection of good coal for locomotives of specific types or for special duties. All engines thus received the same, broken up mixture. Coaling plants like this were common on the LMS and LNER, and the SR had one at Nine Elms and another at Exmouth Junction.

Other depots delivered coal to locomotives by means of skips. Usually there was an inclined ramp up which an aged, small tank engine would push coal wagons which were then unloaded by shovel into individual skips. When a locomotive arrived for coaling, several skips were discharged by tipping their contents into a chute which fed the coal into the tender. Other staff standing on the tender would distribute the coal into the most effective stack shape. This was quite a labour-intensive method, but it was a very common one. All railways used variations of this type of coal stage, even the Great Western at its largest depot, Old Oak Common.

Yet another coaling method used a swing jib crane. Again, wagons in a nearby siding were emptied by shovel into skips. Each was lifted by crane to the tender being filled. Usually by pulling a lever at the back of the skip, a man would open its bottom door and the coal would cascade into the area required. At least this method ensured better placement of the coal in the tender, but it was a slow business to load five or six tons, and also was labour intensive. It was distinctly unpleasant in cold or wet weather!

Discharging ash from the ashpan at the end of a diagram's work was another regular and time-consuming task. Modern locomotives had rocking and drop grates to enable ash and clinker to be more easily broken up and then dropped from the firebox into the ashpan. Nonetheless, rodding out an ashpan to ensure all ash was dropped into a pit was a singularly unpleasant task. Usually another man had to come along later, often with a shovel and wheelbarrow, to dig out the ash from the pit and transfer it to a wagon for final disposal. Ash was used widely in the formation of depot yard surfaces and footpaths, but beware the unwary from treading on ash floating over a flooded manhole or hydrant!

To prevent boilers from scaling up it was necessary to wash out the water passages therein, particularly those around the firebox. This was sensibly achieved when the boiler had cooled. Washout plugs were removed and water hoses were applied through each plug in turn, until the discharge from the lowest plugs was clean.

While ashpans, fireboxes, smokeboxes, coal bunkers and water tanks needed frequent attention, steam locomotives required basic maintenance at intervals from a few days to several weeks. The maintenance of steam locomotives was the responsibility of the depots to which they were allocated. Mechanical maintenance was usually under a specialist mechanical foreman. His gangs of fitters and mates tackled almost anything, other than boiler repairs, the boilermakers' job. Repairs to engines varied widely from replacing leaking steam glands, through renewing worn brake blocks and cleaning out injectors to get them going again, to the really heavy work of lifting an engine to remove axleboxes for remetalling. To ensure that no impending problem was overlooked, the locomotives underwent a series of inspections at regular intervals of days, weeks and months. The really skilled work included ensuring that piston valves or slide valves were properly set so that steam input to, and exhaust from, the cylinders were timed correctly.

Inside a large engine shed were, typically, parallel tracks with shallow pits between the rails. Usually one or two tracks were designated as washout roads, and others were either for stabling, preparation or repairs. Principal depots usually had a small bay or separate shop with lifting equipment: a sheerlegs hoist, jacks or, in extremely well equipped cases such as Old Oak Common, a heavy overhead crane. Sometimes this was backed by a small group of machine tools such as lathes, a shaper and a boring machine.

The larger motive power depots also stabled and looked after a breakdown train. These consisted generally of a stores and packing van, a staff vehicle and a 30- or 45-ton steam breakdown crane. When a derailment occurred (in the days of many small, loose-coupled wagons derailments were frequent, particularly in marshalling yards) the extraction of men from the depot to man the breakdown train often left only a skeleton staff to continue maintenance or repair of the engines there.

One of the more psychologically rewarding activities at a steam depot was engine cleaning, the starting grade in the footplate line of promotion. Locomotives got cleaned if they were able to be stopped on days (young people were barred from shift working), if they could be spared from train running, and if there were sufficient cleaning staff available. Otherwise things just became dirtier! Normally a priority system emerged at a depot, the top link passenger engines getting adequate cleaning while freight and yard pilots were often left uncleaned.

After about 50,000-90,000 miles of running, the axleboxes and horns of a steam locomotive became slack, piston rings often wore and let steam by, frame stretchers and motion brackets began to work loose and in some cases cracks began to appear in the main frames. Sorting out these problems presented a volume and standard of work beyond the capability of depots.

The main works to which engines were sent for overhaul were dominated by high, long erecting shops, surrounded by other shops undertaking boiler and tender repairs and component repair and manufacture. There were machine shops, fitting shops, forges, smithies and foundries. Shops specialised in wheels, brasswork, tool repairs and patternmaking. The works were supported by large stores, amenity blocks including canteens, production offices and management and accountancy sections. The main shops were noisy hives of activity, and totally fascinating to a visitor from the world outside.

At an intermediate overhaul, a locomotive would be pushed into the erecting shop, separated from its tender and moved by overhead cranes to a stripping bay. Here its rods and valve gear were dismantled and its brakework, cab and boiler fittings removed. Two overhead cranes, usually of 50-60 tons capacity each and supported on runways at eaves level along the shop, picked up the locomotive (still carrying its boiler) leaving its wheels and axleboxes behind, and trundled off down the shop with it, slewing it to one side so as to lower it carefully onto prepared stands. Here, during the next week and a few days, it received overhauled injectors, cab and boiler fittings. Any fractures were welded up, loose bolts tightened, horn liners replaced or adjusted for clearance and the frames were cleaned. Paintwork was usually touched up. If cylinders needed reboring, this was done using a rig clamped to the cylinder.

Meanwhile, the wheels had gone off to the wheel shop to have their tyres turned or replaced by new. Bearing surfaces needing attention were skimmed and polished, as were the bosses for coupling and connecting rods. Coupled wheels from high speed engines were placed in a balancing machine and spun, to check and correct any tendency to imbalance following repair. Lead was either added to or removed from the balance weight pockets in the wheels. Axleboxes requiring remetalling were turned upside down, and molten white metal poured into a mould clamped to the box. The axleboxes were then trucked to the machine shop for the rough cast white metal to be machined to a smooth surface, and the oil channels cut in.

Other components such as coupling and connecting rods and valve gear, brake cylinders and rodding, and piston valves, went to a fitting shop for new or remetalled bushes, and new piston rings to be fitted.

Eventually, the repaired bits and pieces came back together in the erecting shop and the locomotive was reassembled, the major operation of lowering down onto the wheels (and later the bogies) being carried out with care and precision. The engine was then lifted onto small rollers to enable the coupled wheels to be levered round to facilitate valve setting.

Once shunted out of the erecting shop, a short run light in steam was a common practice, to ensure all bearings and bushes were free from binding and that any steam leaks were noted and eliminated.

When the second or third major overhaul in a sequence was due, often after about five years of running, a steam locomotive received a general overhaul. The principal difference from the intermediate overhaul described before was that the boiler was removed from the frames, stripped of its lagging and mountings, and given a very thorough inspection and overhaul. Repairs arising from the inspection normally included some re-staying and retubing, and recaulking of joints or stay heads. They frequently went as far as cutting out and welding in, or riveting on, patches to replace wasted areas, or even fitting a complete new firebox or tubeplate. When repairs to a boiler were complete, it would be taken to a stand outside the shop, its openings fitted with blanking plates, and the boiler subjected to hydraulic pressure to a level more than double its maximum working pressure. Water hydraulic testing was the safest method because leaks would be immediately visible and if disaster should unluckily strike, no explosion could result. After any repairs had been carried out, a fire would be lit under the firebox, and the boiler subjected to a steam test to a higher pressure than the working pressure. Only after repairs arising from that test had been completed and proven, was the boiler considered ready to be returned to the erecting shop for placement on a locomotive's frames.

Towards the end of a general repair the complete locomotive was repainted, then taken outside and given a static steam test before its trial run. On return to its home depot, this gleaming apparition would soon gather a thin film of workaday dirt, and only weeks later would be scarcely distinguishable from its colleagues!

Locomotive Works in 1948

Eastern Region:
  Doncaster*
  Stratford
  Gorton

London Midland Region:
  Derby*
  Crewe*
  Horwich*
  Bow

North Eastern Region:
  Darlington*

Scottish Region:
  Saint Rollox
  Cowlairs
  Inverurie
  Loch Gorm

Southern Region:
  Eastleigh*
  Ashford
  Brighton*
  Ryde (IoW)

Western Region:
  Swindon*
  Wolverhampton
  Caerphilly
  Newton Abbot
  Oswestry

*Works still undertaking new building of steam traction as well as overhauls.

The heaviest work on steam locomotives was undertaken at the main workshops such as Eastleigh, where a newly rebuilt 'West Country' 4-6-2 is seen being lowered on to its wheels. *Colin Boocock*

Above:
A new Class 9F 2-10-0 is under construction in the great erecting shop at Swindon. This works produced the last new steam locomotive for BR in 1960. *Colin Boocock*

Below:
The vastness of the Swindon Works 'A Shop' displays locomotives Nos 75003, 1029, 6029, 7015 and 70027, and many others. A traverser ran the length of the shop enabling locomotives to be placed into each bay.
T. B. Owen/Colour-Rail BRW685

Left:
At major cities to which ran more than one of the pre-Grouping railways, even in BR days there was often a separate locomotive depot for each former railway's stock. Bristol was no exception, where the former LMS depot was this one, at Barrow Road, where GW visitors were lately common. *P. W. Gray/Colour-Rail BRM771*

Left:
Former Great Western Railway 'Star' class 4-6-0, No 4061 *Glastonbury Abbey* stands on the turntable in one of the Old Oak Common roundhouses in September 1955. *T. B. Owen/Colour-Rail BRW414*

Below:
The Great Western preferred roundhouses for its major depots, such as this view of engines around one of the turntables in Swindon depot. Included in the picture are Nos 2244, 9773, 4178 and 9605. *A. E. Doyle/Colour-Rail BRW386*

Above:
A large depot could often display a huge variety of steam locomotives. This was the scene at Eastleigh shed yard in the untypical days of the 1955 ASLEF strike.
S. C. Townroe/Colour-Rail BRS336

Left:
Home for the Killin branch engine was this small shed at Loch Tay. This scene shows Caledonian 0-4-4T No 55217 being prepared for a day's branch line service in April 1961. *D. M. C. Hepburne-Scott/Colour-Rail SC344*

Top right:
Under the coaling plant at Perth motive power depot in 1959 stands red 'Coronation' Pacific No 46247 *City of Liverpool*.
W. J. V. Anderson/Colour-Rail SC120

Bottom right:
Seven locomotives are grouped around the turntable in Ebbw Junction roundhouse in September 1963.
T. B. Owen/Colour-Rail BRW534

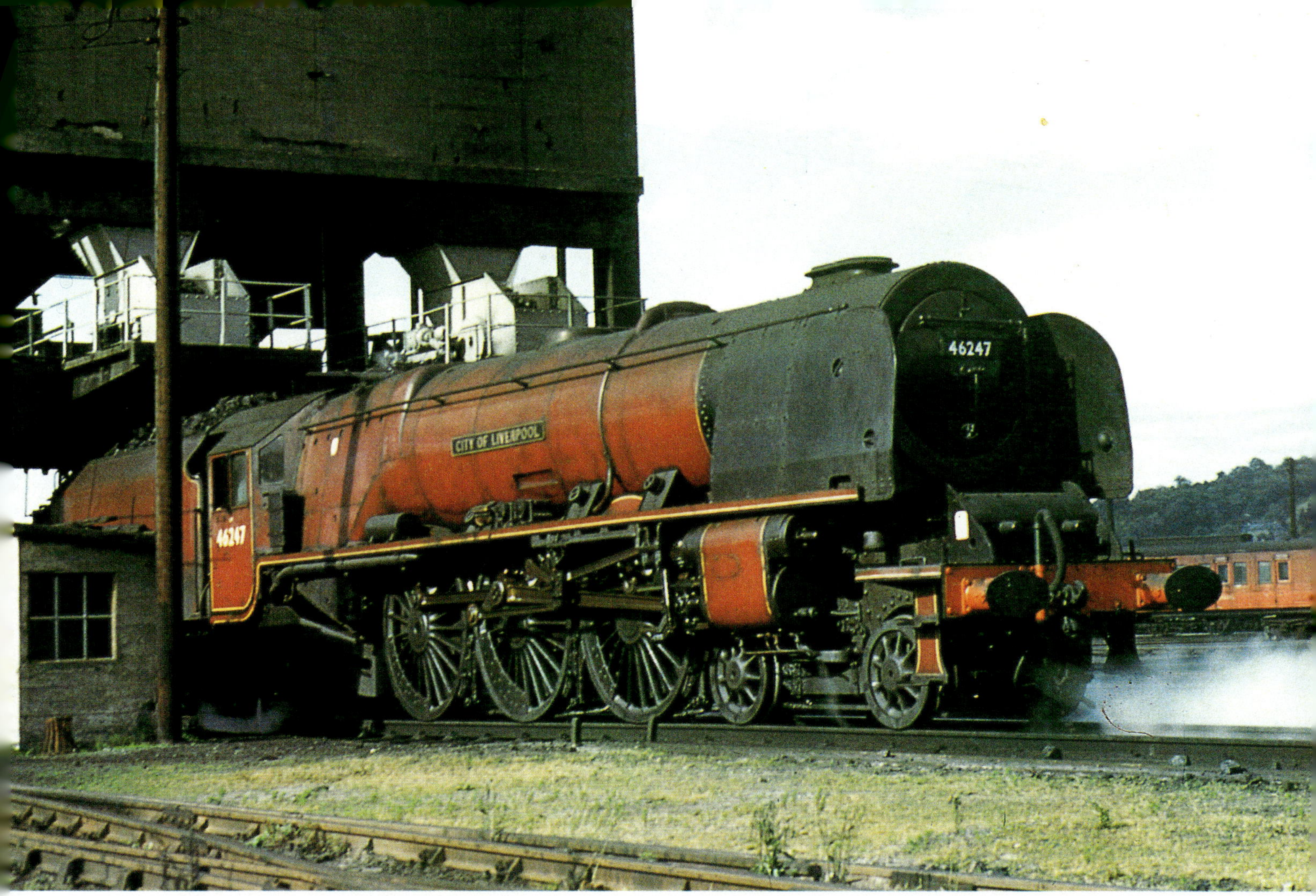
46247
CITY OF LIVERPOOL
46247

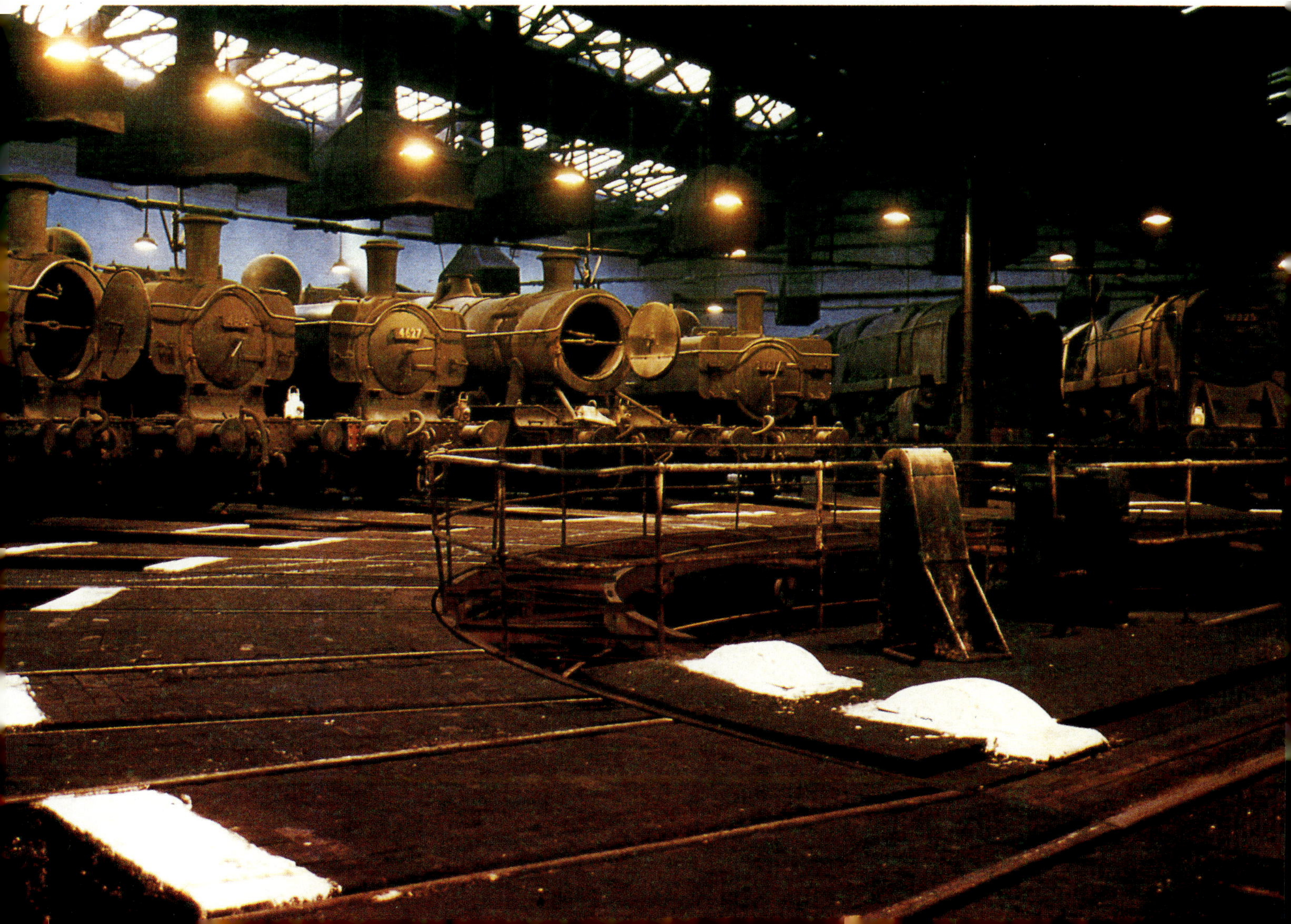

Barrow Road shed yard is crowded as locomotives await attention one evening in 1961.
T. B. Owen/Colour-Rail BRM549

Nos 45592 *Indore* and 46148 *The Manchester Regiment* pose outside Camden depot, London, in 1962.
J. G. Dewing/Colour-Rail BRM772

Above:
This LMS line-up in 1958 at Kentish Town shed comprises Class 5 No 44822, '4F' 0-6-0 No 44563, '2P' 4-4-0 No 40413 and 'Jubilee' No 45724 *Warspite*.
T. B. Owen/Colour-Rail BRM551

Left:
One of the many medium sized depots in the industrial north was Barnsley, seen in August 1959.
G. Warnes/Colour-Rail BRE521

Left:
In 1961 it was possible to see 'A3s' with German-style smoke deflectors in large numbers. Two of them, Nos 60062 *Minoru* and 60039 *Sandwich*, flank engines Nos 60025 *Falcon*, 60906, and 60028 *Walter K. Whigham* at King's Cross 'Top Shed'. *P. Mullett/Colour-Rail BRE320*

NINE

STEAM'S LAST STAND

Two events combined to accelerate the decline and fall of the steam locomotive on British Railways. Firstly, there was the political support for the speeding up of diesel locomotive and multiple-unit deliveries in the late 1950s. Secondly, when the route rationalisations following the Beeching reports made their impact in the mid-1960s, the number of locomotives required for traffic on BR fell very rapidly. Consequently, the latest steam locomotives built had very short lives. The first BR Standard locomotive was delivered in 1951, the last in 1960. All had gone by late 1968, and no BR Standard engine lasted more than 17 years. Many saw as little as seven years' active service.

When sufficient diesels had been delivered to make an impact on the principal routes, there developed a policy of blanket dieselisation of certain large areas. Thus the Liverpool Street division of the Eastern Region became the first on BR to be fully cleared of steam operation, other than of services penetrating into it. The Western was the first Region to lose its allocated steam locomotives. In no way did the choices reflect the quality or age of the engines there. It was the nature and direction of the spread of modern traction which caused the former Great Western types to be the first pre-Nationalisation engines to be eliminated from the rails of BR. This occurred in the winter of 1964/65.

In the other Regions, the few remaining pre-Grouping classes disappeared first, with the notable exception of the North Eastern Railway 'Q6' and 'J27' locomotives. These survived as late as 1966 on their home ground in Tees and Tyneside, probably a full four years beyond most other pre-1923 classes, of which a few ex-LBSCR 0-6-2Ts were among the last to go in the SR's purge of 1962.

What certainly did not happen, as many had supposed would be the case, was the expected survival of BR Standard designs beyond all the Regional types. In almost every area that lost its steam traction, Regional classes were prominent among the last survivors. This was not surprising on the Western where BR types had scarcely become popular, nor on the East Coast main line where Gresley, Thompson and Peppercorn Pacifics kept all the top jobs until ousted by the 'Deltics' and other diesel-electrics. But on the Southern's South Eastern division, for example, electrification and dieselisation merely served to push 'Schools' and

Moguls farther west, and in Scotland, displaced 'A4s' exploited their potential when they took over the Glasgow-Aberdeen run. The author is not aware of any division or district on BR which ever became totally dependent on BR Standard steam locomotives for its operations.

Many observers have commented that towards the end of steam, locomotives became run-down as a result of a decline in maintenance and cleaning standards. While this clearly did happen in some depots, and indeed there is a sound psychological reason why this might have been so, it was in fact by no means universally the case. Certainly some Western locomotives reached a very sad visual state: cabside numberplates, nameplates and even the brass safety valve covers, were sometimes seen to be missing, signs that they were no longer loved. It had never been uncommon to see dirty engines on the London Midland and Eastern Regions, but some of the steam leaks that escaped attention in the last couple of years in some places did border on the excessive. The pictures which accompany this chapter are a fair cross-section of what could be seen in the last four years of steam operation on BR. They include some reminders that many depots kept their engines clean and mechanically 'tight' right up to the end.

The last main line to use steam locomotives on top link passenger turns was that from Waterloo to Bournemouth and Weymouth. 1967 was the year, and enthusiast attention to the route was high, reaching a crescendo in the few weeks before the last day on 9 July. For several years before, the SR had set up Guildford depot as a centre for specialist maintenance work such as valves and pistons examinations. To an extent as a result of this work, the mechanical condition of Southern engines actually improved. Thus there were many excellent performances possible from the last rebuilt 'Merchant Navy' and 'West Country' locomotives in the hands of drivers having a last fling: 100mph running was reported by the travelling fans on several occasions. Even the few remaining unrebuilt Bulleid Pacifics did some good running, backed by the ever-willing BR Standard Class 5s. The only sad sign of the impending end of the work of the steam engine cleaner was the layer of grime which spread across these great steam machines in the last months of their extremely active lives. Even that had its advantage to a few. It was more effective than shiny paint as a base for the inevitable chalked epitaphs which adorned the last steam locomotives on their last runs!

A feature of these years was the heightening popularity of special trains for enthusiasts. In the early 1960s the object of many tours had been visits to closing branch lines or secondary routes. Now the emphasis was on a last chance to ride behind a favourite steam locomotive, or to parade an engine in areas which it had never visited before. Thus an 'A3' went to Bournemouth, an 'A4' visited Weymouth, and a 'Merchant Navy' broke records on the climb to Ais Gill summit. One can recall more than one last chance to ride behind a 'Castle'! The official 'last steam' runs to Bournemouth were held at least a week before the actual last day!

When the Southern's last steam engines had made their final, funereal trips to Weymouth and Salisbury depots in the dark of that Sunday night in July 1967, there remained only one area worked by steam on BR. The lines radiating from Preston and Manchester, fed by the depots at Carnforth, Lostock Hall and Buxton, became the pilgrim centre for steam fans. Thus the last steam enthusiasts concentrated their massed cameras on stone trains being hauled up the Pennines by clanking '8Fs' in the snow, or they waited for a less-than-certain Class 5 to appear on a local passenger train at Preston. The last steam locomotives on BR were mostly LMS Class 5s and '8Fs', with a few Standard Class 4s and 5s supporting them. Crewe works surprisingly outshopped No 70013 *Oliver Cromwell*

after a late overhaul, but did not line out its green paintwork.

Then came the last specials, the end of steam on British Rail. A high fare was charged, but many paid to ride behind No 70013, and behind a pair of 'Black 5s', Nos 44871 and 44781, and lastly behind No 45110. Then everyone believed it was all over.

During these years the merchants whose yards scrapped old railway equipment had been having a boom time. The last years saw thousands of engines broken up for scrap. Visitors to these places saw their favourites standing gaunt, rusty, and with signs that the cutter's torch had begun its work. The value of scrap copper and steel enhanced the urgency of the work. In a remarkably short time most of the relics had disappeared, cut into unrecognisable chunks of twisted metal and dropped into some blast furnace somewhere to be recycled, most likely as not to become cars or washing machines — except at one location in Wales.

Maybe it was the slower pace of life in that principality, or maybe Dai Woodham had his eye on an investment: whatever the reason, over 200 steam locomotives stood on the site of Woodham's scrapyard on Barry Island and most escaped the torch. A few engines had been purchased directly from British Rail by steam railways and individuals, but the story of how and why one man saved so many more for posterity will no doubt be told in good time.

Above:
As the twilight of steam's reign on British Railways approaches, red Pacific No 46256 *Sir William A. Stanier, FRS* stands under the wires at Glasgow Central in April 1964. *D. Cameron/Colour-Rail SC195*

Top right:
This pre-Grouping 0-6-0 had been repainted as late as 1966! Class J27 No 65842 is seen at Woodburn with the Thursdays only goods from Morpeth in September of that year. *J. M. Boyes/Colour-Rail BRE222*

Bottom right:
Two outwardly ill-kempt BR Class 4 4-6-0s Nos 75053 and 75063, make a fine picture as they breast Talerddig summit in December 1965 with the up 'Cambrian Coast Express'. *T. B. Owen/Colour-Rail BRW517*

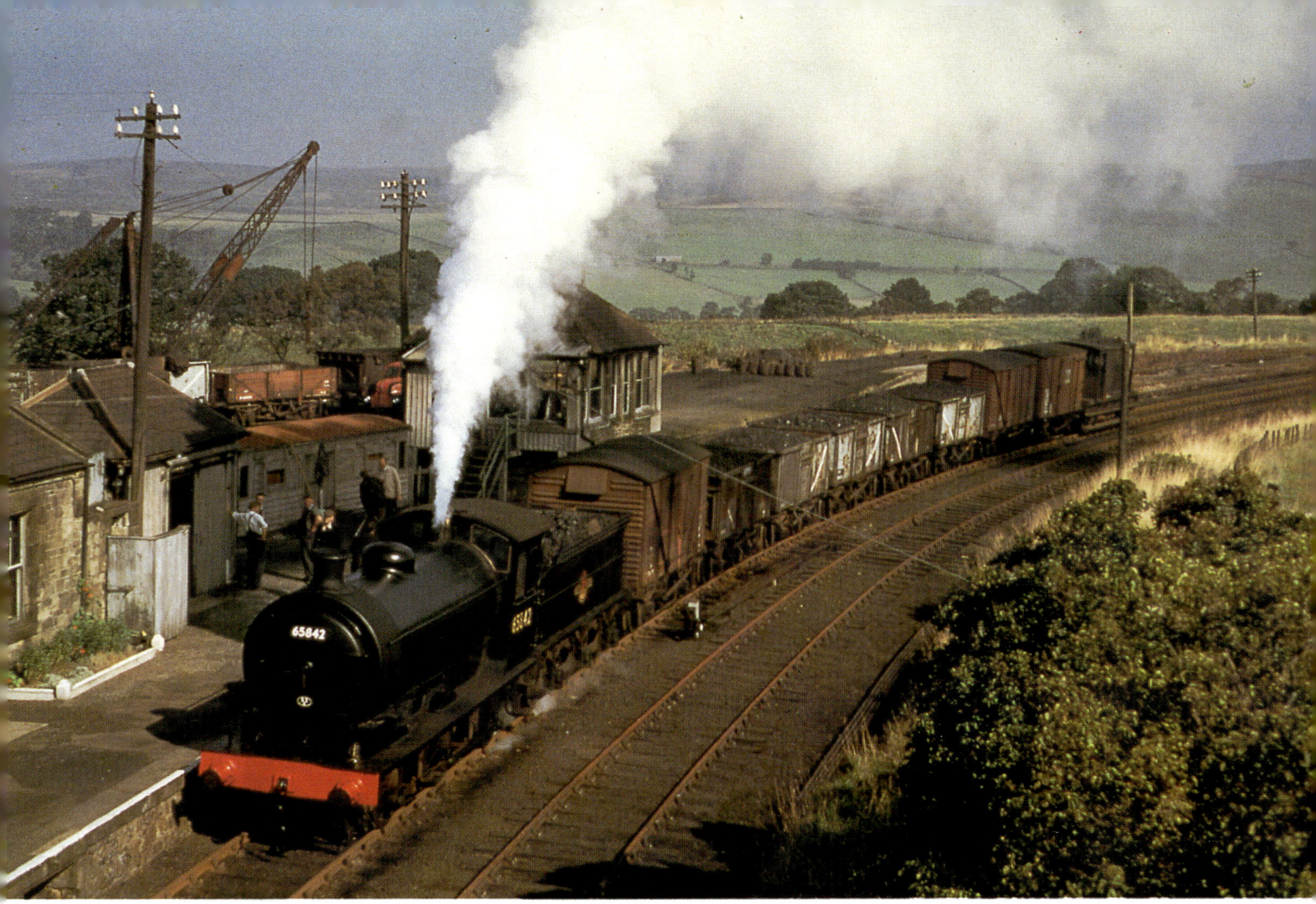
65842

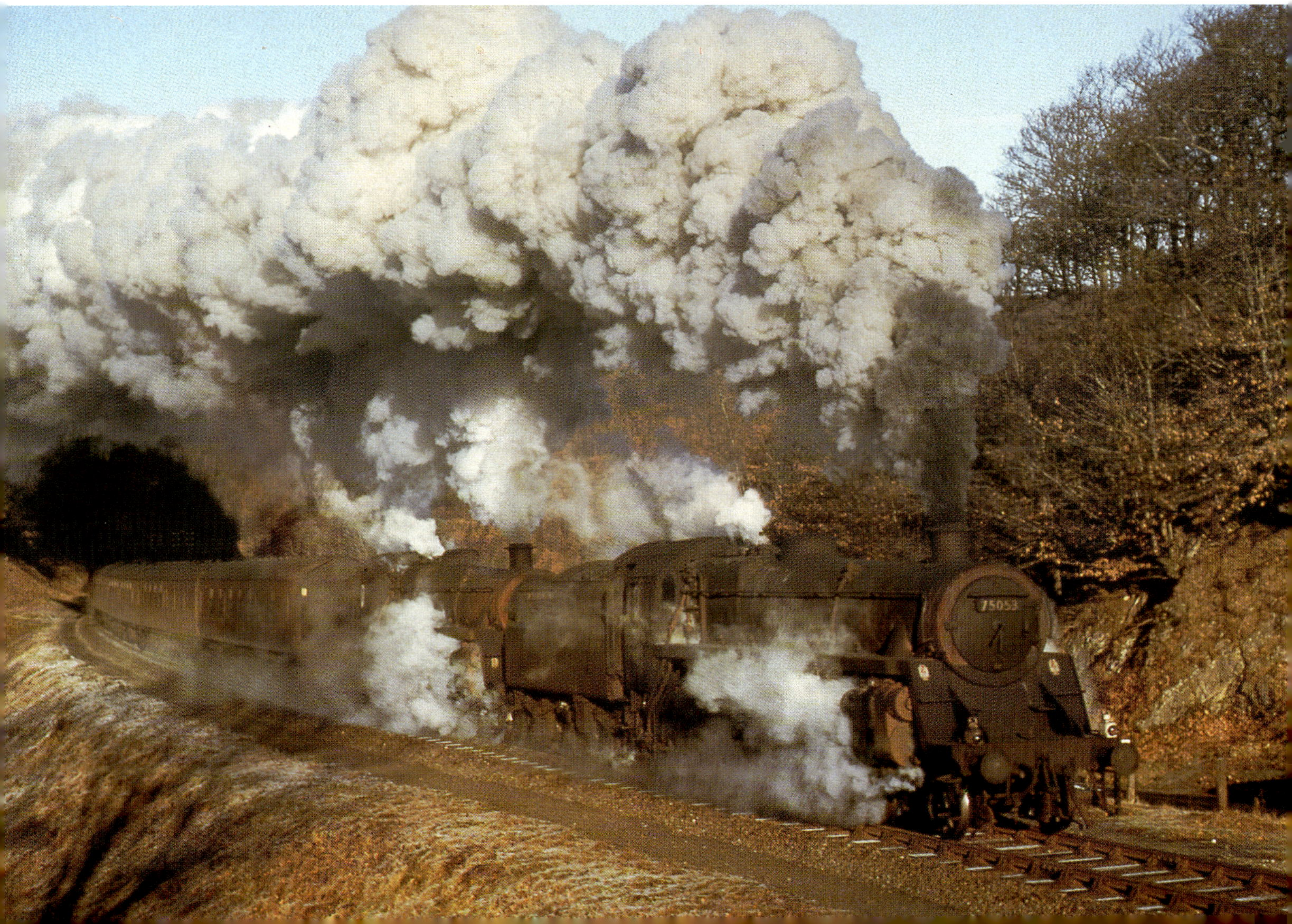
75053

Steam reigned supreme in the North-west while other areas succumbed to diesel or electric traction. On Ais Gill Viaduct, 2-10-0 No 92017 heads an up freight in September 1965.
A. E. R. Cope/Colour-Rail BRM536

Class 5 4-6-0 No 44795 surmounts the summit of the Settle & Carlisle line at Ais Gill with a freight in May 1966.
A. E. R. Cope/Colour-Rail BRM 193

Above:
A feature of the last months of steam working was the appearance of engines well away from their normal spheres of operation, as available motive power was used to the best advantage. This strange face at Doncaster is 'Black 5' No 45208 which had arrived in February 1967 with the 20.20 from Bradford. *G. Warnes/Colour-Rail BRE517*

Below:
St Pancras station is the background to this classic shot of 'Jubilee' 4-6-0 No 45721 *Impregnable* awaiting departure with an enthusiasts' special. *R. Hill/Colour-Rail BRM161*

Above:
December 1964 produced sufficient snow for this delightful scene on the Cambrian main line. Ex-GW 4-6-0 No 7827 *Lydham Manor* climbs towards Talerddig with the up 'Cambrian Coast Express'. *T. B. Owen/Colour-Rail BRW450*

Left:
Extreme cold weather was not ideal for efficient steam locomotive operation! In this photograph taken in the winter of 1963, BR Class 5 4-6-0 No 73093 appears to be in control as it starts an up local on the former LSWR main line at Farnborough. *T. B. Owen/Colour-Rail BRS431*

Left:
Preston was one of the last major BR stations to be served by steam. In its LNW trainshed. Class 5 4-6-0 No 44892 pauses with a parcels train in February 1966.
B. Magilton/Colour-Rail BRM601

The Isle of Wight system retained steam operation with ex-LSWR Class O2 0-4-4Ts right up to electrification in 1966. Not long before the end of steam there, No W22 *Brading* climbs past Smallbrook Junction near Ryde with a train for the Shanklin line. *J. G. Dewing/Colour-Rail BRS478*

In the summer of 1964 another load of holidaymakers going south in the 'Pines Express' to Bournemouth are hauled at speed past Shawford by clean rebuilt 'West Country' 4-6-2 No 34017 *Ilfracombe.* *B. J. Swain/Colour-Rail BRS425*

Above:
Many BR tank engines were sold to other concerns when no longer required. Among these was GW pannier tank No 7760 which became No L90 of London Transport, seen here shunting at Watford tip in January 1968.
P. Zabek/Colour-Rail LT19

Left:
No 80103 was the first BR Class 4 2-6-4T to be withdrawn for scrap. It stands here forlorn, at the head of a row of ex-Great Eastern 'J15' 0-6-0s at Stratford in 1962.
Colin Boocock

Left:
All-out effort! LMS Class 8F 2-8-0 No 48532 makes an explosively evocative sight (not to say sound) as it heads a Tunstead empty stone train near Buxworth in February 1968. *W. Chapman/Colour-Rail BRM541*

APPENDICES
1 British Railways Steam Classes 1948 and 1961

Ex-LNER types

Class	Wheel Arrangement	Origin	Number in Class 1948	Number in Class 1961
A1	4-6-2	LNER/BR	4	50
A2	4-6-2	LNER	40	30
A3	4-6-2	LNER	77	76
A4	4-6-2	LNER	34	34
A5	4-6-2T	GCR	43	—
A6	4-6-2T	NER	9	—
A7	4-6-2T	NER	20	—
A8	4-6-2T	NER	45	—
A10	4-6-2	GNR	1	—
B1	4-6-0	LNER	340	409
B2	4-6-0	LNER	9	—
B3	4-6-0	GCR	1	—
B4	4-6-0	GCR	4	—
B5	4-6-0	GCR	4	—
B7	4-6-0	GCR	25	—
B8	4-6-0	GCR	2	—
B9	4-6-0	GCR	3	—
B12	4-6-0	GER	71	1
B13	4-6-0	NER	1	—
B16	4-6-0	NER	69	44
B17 'Sandringham'	4-6-0	LNER	64	—
C1	4-4-2	GNR	10	—
C4	4-4-2	GCR	15	—
C7	4-4-2	NER	2	—
C12	4-4-2T	GNR	44	—
C13	4-4-2T	GCR	40	—
C14	4-4-2T	GCR	12	—
C15	4-4-2T	NBR	30	—
C16	4-4-2T	NBR	21	—
D1	4-4-0	GNR	7	—
D2	4-4-0	GNR	26	—
D3	4-4-0	GNR	15	—
D9	4-4-0	GCR	26	—
D10 'Director'	4-4-0	GCR	10	—
D11 'Large Director'	4-4-0	GCR	34	5
D15 'Claud Hamilton'	4-4-0	GER	12	—
D16 'Super Claud'	4-4-0	GER	102	—
D20	4-4-0	NER	49	—
D29 'Scott'	4-4-0	NBR	10	—
D30 'Scott'	4-4-0	NBR	25	—
D31	4-4-0	NBR	4	—
D32	4-4-0	NBR	5	—
D33	4-4-0	NBR	9	—
D34 'Glen'	4-4-0	NBR	30	3
D40	4-4-0	GNSR	18	1
D41	4-4-0	GNSR	21	—
D49 'Shire'/'Hunt'	4-4-0	LNER	76	—
E4	2-4-0	GER	18	—
F1	2-4-2T	MSLR	2	—
F2	2-4-2T	GCR	8	—
F3	2-4-2T	GER	8	—
F4	2-4-2T	GER	26	—
F5	2-4-2T	GER	30	—

Class	Wheel Arrangement	Origin	Number in Class 1948	Number in Class 1961
F6	2-4-2T	GER	22	—
F7	2-4-2T	GER	2	—
G5	0-4-4T	NER	109	—
J1	0-6-0	GNR	11	—
J2	0-6-0	GNR	9	—
J3	0-6-0	GNR	30	—
J4	0-6-0	GNR	4	—
J5	0-6-0	GNR	20	—
J6	0-6-0	GNR	110	10
J10	0-6-0	MSLR	77	2
J11	0-6-0	GCR	174	33
J15	0-6-0	GER	116	14
J17	0-6-0	GER	89	15
J19	0-6-0	GER	35	8
J20	0-6-0	GER	25	9
J21	0-6-0	NER	77	2
J24	0-6-0	NER	31	—
J25	0-6-0	NER	74	9
J26	0-6-0	NER	50	17
J27	0-6-0	NER	115	92
J35	0-6-0	NBR	70	5
J36	0-6-0	NBR	118	69
J37	0-6-0	NBR	104	98
J38	0-6-0	LNER	35	35
J39	0-6-0	LNER	289	141
J50	0-6-0T	GNR	102	40
J52	0-6-0ST	GNR	133	—
J55	0-6-0ST	GNR	2	—
J62	0-6-0ST	GCR	3	—
J63	0-6-0T	GCR	7	—
J65	0-6-0T	GER	3	—
J66	0-6-0T	GER	19	1
J67	0-6-0T	GER	45	—
J68	0-6-0T	GER	29	3
J69	0-6-0T	GER	89	20
J70	0-6-0Tram	GER	11	—
J71	0-6-0T	NER	81	—
J72	0-6-0T	NER	81	59
J73	0-6-0T	NER	10	—
J75	0-6-0T	HBR	1	—
J77	0-6-0T	NER	45	—
J83	0-6-0T	NBR	39	11
J88	0-6-0T	NBR	35	8
J92	0-6-0CT	GER	3	—
J93	0-6-0T	MGNJR	1	—
J94	0-6-0ST	WD	75	66
K1	2-6-0	LNER/BR	1	70
K2	2-6-0	GNR	75	3
K3	2-6-0	LNER	192	142
K4	2-6-0	LNER	5	5
K5	2-6-0	LNER	1	—
L1	2-6-4T	LNER	30	79
L2	2-6-4T	Met	2	—
L3	2-6-4T	GCR	19	—
M2	0-6-4T	Met	2	—
N1	0-6-2T	GNR	55	

Class	Wheel Arrangement	Origin	Number in Class 1948	1961
N2	0-6-2T	GNR	107	20
N4	0-6-2T	MSLR	22	—
N5	0-6-2T	MSLR	121	—
N7	0-6-2T	GER	134	25
N8	0-6-2T	NER	30	—
N9	0-6-2T	NER	16	—
N10	0-6-2T	NER	20	3
N13	0-6-2T	HBR	9	—
N14	0-6-2T	NBR	3	—
N15	0-6-2T	NBR	99	24
O1	2-8-0	GCR/LNER	52	58
O2	2-8-0	GNR	66	56
O3	2-8-0	GNR	15	—
O4	2-8-0	GCR	277	202
O7*	2-8-0	WD	200	—
Q1	0-8-0T	GCR	13	—
Q4	0-8-0	GCR	34	—
Q5	0-8-0	NER	66	—
Q6	0-8-0	NER	120	119
Q7	0-8-0	NER	15	15
S1	0-8-4T	GCR	6	—
T1	4-8-0T	NER	13	—
U1	2-8-0+0-8-2T	LNER	1	—
V1	2-6-2T	LNER	78	17
V2	2-6-2	LNER	184	184
V3	2-6-2T	LNER	14	67
V4	2-6-2	LNER	2	—
W1	4-6-4	LNER	1	—
Y1	0-4-0T	Sentinel	23	1
Y3	0-4-0T	Sentinel	31	3
Y4	0-4-0T	GER	5	1
Y6	0-4-0Tram	GER	2	—
Y7	0-4-0T	NER	2	—
Y8	0-4-0T	NER	2	—
Y9	0-4-0ST	NBR	33	6
Y10	0-4-0T	Sentinel	1	—
Z4	0-4-2T	GNSR	2	—
Z5	0-4-2T	GNSR	2	—

Number of classes: 146 55

Number of locomotives: 6,124 2,520

*See also WD 2-8-0, ex-War Department classes.

Key:

BR	British Railways
GCR	Great Central Railway
GER	Great Eastern Railway
GNR	Great Northern Railway
GNSR	Great North of Scotland Railway
HBR	Hull & Barnsley Railway
LNER	London & North Eastern Railway
Met	Metropolitan Railway
MGNJR	Midland & Great Northern Joint Railway
MSLR	Manchester, Sheffield & Lincoln Railway
NBR	North British Railway
NER	North Eastern Railway
WD	War Department

Ex-LMS types

Class	Wheel Arrangement	Origin	1948	1961
7P/8P 'Princess Royal'	4-6-2	LMS	13	12
7P/8P 'Coronation'	4-6-2	LMS	38	38
6P/7P 'Rebuilt Scot'	4-6-0	LMS	47	71
6P/7P 'Royal Scot'	4-6-0	LMS	24	—
6P/7P 'Rebuilt Jubilee'	4-6-0	LMS	2	2
6P/7P 'Rebuilt Patriot'	4-6-0	LMS	10	17

Class	Wheel Arrangement	Origin	Number in Class 1948	1961
5XP/6P 'Jubilee'	4-6-0	LMS	189	185
5XP/6P 'Patriot'	4-6-0	LMS	42	27
5XP 'Claughton'	4-6-0	LNWR	1	—
5	4-6-0	LMS	802	842
5P	4-6-0	LYR	5	—
4P 'Prince of Wales'	4-6-0	LNWR	3	—
4F Whale '19in Goods'	4-6-0	LNWR	3	—
4P	4-6-0	CR	5	—
4P	4-6-0	LMS/CR	14	—
4P 'Clan'	4-6-0	HR	1	—
4F 'Clan Goods'	4-6-0	HR	6	—
4P 'Compound'	4-4-0	MR	40	1
4P 'Compound'	4-4-0	LMS	195	—
3P 'Precursor'	4-4-0	LNWR	1	—
3P	4-4-0	MR	18	—
3P Class 928	4-4-0	CR	16	4
3P Class 72	4-4-0	CR	32	13
3P 'Dunalastair IV' rebuilt	4-4-0	CR	2	—
3P 'Dunalastair IV'	4-4-0	CR	20	—
2P	4-4-0	MR	165	3
2P	4-4-0	LMS	136	49
2P	4-4-0	CR	1	—
2P 'Loch'	4-4-0	HR	1	—
2P 'Ben'	4-4-0	HR	8	—
— Beyer Garratt	2-6-0+0-6-2T	LMS	33	—
—	0-10-0	MR	1	—
8F	2-8-0	LMS	624	665
7F	2-8-0	SDJR	11	7
5F Hughes	2-6-0	LMS	245	242
5F Stanier	2-6-0	LMS	40	40
4F Ivatt	2-6-0	LMS	40	162
2F Ivatt	2-6-0	LMS	35	128
1P 6ft 9in	2-4-0	MR	1	—
1P 6ft 3in	2-4-0	MR	1	—
7F	0-8-0	LMS	175	4
7F G2a	0-8-0	LNWR	320	90
7F G2	0-8-0	LNWR	60	41
6F G1	0-8-0	LNWR	98	—
7F	0-8-0	LYR	14	—
6F	0-8-0	LYR	11	—
4F	0-6-0	MR	192	100
4F	0-6-0	LMS	580	482
3F Aspinall	0-6-0	LYR	235	1
3F Hughes	0-6-0	LYR	35	17
3F	0-6-0	MR	11	1
3F	0-6-0	SDJR	9	1
3F Johnson	0-6-0	MR	317	61
3F Deeley	0-6-0	MR	54	7
3F	0-6-0	FR	6	—
3F Class 812/652	0-6-0	CR	89	62
3F Class 294	0-6-0	CR	23	22
3F Class 670	0-6-0	CR	6	6
3F	0-6-0	HR	7	—
2F	0-6-0	LNWR	58	—
2F	0-6-0	LNWR	35	—
2F	0-6-0	LYR	23	—
2F Johnson	0-6-0	MR	95	18
2F Johnson	0-6-0	MR	93	3
2F Kirtley	0-6-0	MR	4	—
2F	0-6-0	CR	222	106
4P	4-6-2T	CR	9	—
3P	4-4-2T	LTSR	51	—
2P	4-4-2T	LTSR	17	—
4P Fairburn	2-6-4T	LMS	180	277
4P Stanier	2-6-4T	LMS	206	202
4P Stanier 3-cyl	2-6-4T	LMS	37	33
4P Fowler	2-6-4T	LMS	125	104
3P Stanier	2-6-2T	LMS	139	120
3P Fowler	2-6-2T	LMS	70	3

Class	Wheel Arrangement	Origin	Number in Class 1948	Number in Class 1961
2P Ivatt	2-6-2T	LMS	30	130
3P	2-4-2T	LYR	8	—
2P	2-4-2T	LYR	105	1
1P	2-4-2T	LNWR	30	—
1P	2-4-0T	LNWR	1	—
7F	0-8-4T	LNWR	10	—
6F	0-8-2T	LNWR	8	—
3F	0-6-2T	LTSR	14	1
2P	0-6-2T	LNWR	9	—
2F	0-6-2T	LNWR	50	—
3F	0-6-0T	LMS	412	325
3F	0-6-0T	MR	60	22
3F	0-6-0T	CR	147	14
2F	0-6-0T	LMS	10	7
2F	0-6-0T	NLR	14	—
2F	0-6-0T	CR	23	2
1F	0-6-0T	LYR	5	1
1F	0-6-0T	MR	87	11
2F	0-6-0ST	LNWR	1	—
2F	0-6-0ST	LYR	95	13
2P	0-4-4T	LMS	10	1
2P	0-4-4T	LMS/CR	10	1
2P Class 431	0-4-4T	CR	4	2
2P Class 439	0-4-4T	CR	74	29
2P Class 19	0-4-4T	CR	24	1
1P	0-4-4T	MR	8	—
1P	0-4-4T	MR	51	—
0P	0-4-4T	HR	2	—
1F	0-4-2ST	LNWR	2	—
—	0-4-2CT	NLR	1	—
0F	0-4-0T	MR	10	5
— Sentinel	0-4-0T	LMS	7	—
— Railmotor	0-4-0T	LNWR	1	—
0F	0-4-0ST	LMS	5	10
0F	0-4-0ST	LYR	23	12
0F	0-4-0ST	MR	3	—
0F	0-4-0ST	CR	14	3
—	4-6-0	HR	—	1
—	4-2-2	CR	—	1

Number of classes: 112 64

Number of locomotives: 7,805 4,862

Key:

CR	Caledonian Railway
FR	Furness Railway
HR	Highland Railway
LMS	London, Midland & Scottish Railway
LNWR	London & North Western Railway
LTSR	London, Tilbury & Southend Railway
LYR	Lancashire & Yorkshire Railway
MR	Midland Railway
SDJR	Somerset & Dorset Joint Railway

Ex-SR Types:

Class	Wheel Arrangement	Origin	Number in Class 1948	Number in Class 1961
A1 'Terrier'	0-6-0T	LBSCR	1	1
A1X 'Terrier'	0-6-0T	LBSCR	14	10
A12	0-4-2	LSWR	2	—
B1	4-4-0	SECR	11	—
B4	0-4-0T	LSWR	22	3
B4	4-4-0	LBSCR	6	—
B4X	4-4-0	LBSCR	12	—
C	0-6-0	SECR	106	38
C2	0-6-0	LBSCR	2	—
C2X	0-6-0	LBSCR	45	20
C3	0-6-0	LBSCR	8	—
C14	0-4-0T	LSWR	3	—
D	4-4-0	SECR	28	—
D1	4-4-0	SECR	20	5
D1	0-4-2T	LBSCR	13	—
D3	0-4-4T	LBSCR	26	—
D15	4-4-0	LSWR	10	—

Class	Wheel Arrangement	Origin	Number in Class 1948	Number in Class 1961
E	4-4-0	SECR	15	—
E1	4-4-0	SECR	11	1
E1	0-6-0T	LBSCR	26	—
E1/R	0-6-2T	LBSCR	10	—
E2	0-6-2T	LBSCR	10	8
E3	0-6-2T	LBSCR	16	—
E4	0-6-2T	LBSCR	70	19
E4X	0-6-2T	LBSCR	4	—
E5	0-6-2T	LBSCR	24	—
E5X	0-6-2T	LBSCR	4	—
E6	0-6-2T	LBSCR	10	5
E6X	0-6-2T	LBSCR	2	—
F1	4-4-0	SECR	4	—
G6	0-6-0T	LSWR	32	2
G16	4-8-0T	LSWR	4	2
H	0-4-4T	SECR	63	21
H1	4-4-2	LBSCR	3	—
H2	4-4-2	LBSCR	6	—
H15	4-6-0	LSWR/SR	26	5
H16	4-6-2T	LSWR	5	5
I1X	4-4-2T	LBSCR	9	—
I3	4-4-2T	LBSCR	26	—
J	0-6-4T	SECR	5	—
J1	4-6-2T	LBSCR	1	—
J2	4-6-2T	LBSCR	1	—
K	2-6-0	LBSCR	17	17
K10	4-4-0	LSWR	23	—
KESR	0-8-0T	KESR	1	—
L	4-4-0	SECR	22	2
L1	4-4-0	SR	15	8
L11	4-4-0	LSWR	40	—
L12	4-4-0	LSWR	20	—
LN 'Lord Nelson'	4-6-0	SR	16	14
M7	0-4-4T	LSWR	103	57
'Merchant Navy'	4-6-2	SR	30	—
'Merchant Navy' rebuilt	4-6-2	SR/BR	—	30
N	2-6-0	SECR	80	80
N1	2-6-0	SECR	6	6
N15 'King Arthur'	4-6-0	LSWR/SR	74	18
N15X 'Remembrance'	4-6-0	LBSCR/SR	7	—
O1	0-6-0	SECR	46	—
O2	0-4-4T	LSWR	48	25
P	0-6-0T	SECR	8	8
Q	0-6-0	SR	20	20
Q1	0-6-0	SR	40	40
R	0-4-4T	SECR	15	—
R1	0-4-4T	SECR	13	—
R1	0-6-0T	SECR	9	—
S	0-6-0ST	SECR	1	—
S11	4-4-0	LSWR	10	—
S15	4-6-0	LSWR/SR	45	45
T	0-6-0T	SECR	3	—
T1	0-4-4T	LSWR	9	—
T9	4-4-0	LSWR	66	2
T14	4-6-0	LSWR	9	—
U	2-6-0	SECR	50	50
U1	2-6-0	SR	21	21
V 'Schools'	4-4-0	SR	40	34
W	2-6-4T	SR	15	15
'West Country'/ 'Battle of Britain'	4-6-2	SR	90	50
'West Country'/ 'Battle of Britain' rebuilt	4-6-2	SR/BR	—	60
Z	0-8-0T	SR	8	8
700	0-6-0	LSWR	30	18
756	0-6-0T	PDSWJR	1	—
757	0-6-2T	PDSWJR	2	—
1302	0-4-0CT	SECR	1	—
0298	2-4-0WT	LSWR	3	3
0395	0-6-0	LSWR	18	—
0458	0-4-0ST	LSWR	1	—
0415	4-4-2T	LSWR	3	—

Class	Wheel Arrangement	Origin	Number in Class 1948	1961
USA	0-6-0T	USATC	14	14
30948	0-6-0T	EKR	1	—
'Leader'	0-6-6-0T	SR/BR	†	—
Number of classes:			87	39
Number of locomotives:			1,810	782

†Five locomotives built (four not commissioned) 1949; all scrapped 1950-51.

Key:

BR	British Railways
EKR	East Kent Railway
KESR	Kent & East Sussex Railway
LBSCR	London, Brighton & South Coast Railway
LSWR	London & South Western Railway
PDSWJR	Plymouth, Devonport & South Western Junction Railway
SECR	South Eastern & Chatham Railway (incorporating South Eastern Railway and London, Chatham & Dover Railway)
SR	Southern Railway
USATC	United States Army Transportation Corps

Ex-GWR Types:

Class	Wheel Arrangement	Origin	Number in Class 1948	1961
517	0-4-2T	GWR	3	—
10XX	4-6-0	GWR	30	30
1101	0-4-0T	GWR	6	—
1361	0-6-0ST	GWR	5	2
1366	0-6-0PT	GWR	6	3
14XX	0-4-2T	GWR	95	28
15XX	0-6-0PT	GWR/BR	—	7
1501	0-6-0PT	GWR	9	—
16XX	0-6-0PT	GWR/BR	—	51
1701	0-6-0PT	GWR	27	—
1813	0-6-0PT	GWR	1	—
1901	0-6-0PT	GWR	44	—
2021	0-6-0PT	GWR	110	—
2251	0-0-0	GWR	120	80
2301	0-6-0	GWR	53	—
26XX 'Aberdare'	2-6-0	GWR	4	—
27XX	0-6-0PT	GWR	40	—
28XX	2-8-0	GWR	167	117
29XX 'Saint'	4-6-0	GWR	41	—
31XX	2-6-2T	GWR	5	—
3150	2-6-2T	GWR	30	—
3252 'Duke'	4-4-0	GWR	11	—
33XX 'Bulldog'	4-4-0	GWR	34	—
35XX	2-4-0T	GWR	7	—
40XX 'Star'	4-6-0	GWR	46	—
4073 'Castle'	4-6-0	GWR	151	155
42XX	2-8-0T	GWR	151	130
43XX	2-6-0	GWR	235	121
44XX	2-6-2T	GWR	11	—
45XX	2-6-2T	GWR	175	53
47XX	2-8-0	GWR	9	9
49XX 'Hall'	4-6-0	GWR	258	251
51XX	2-6-2T	GWR	148	96
54XX	0-6-0PT	GWR	25	5
56XX	0-6-2T	GWR	200	200
57XX	0-6-0PT	GWR	831	608
60XX 'King'	4-6-0	GWR	30	30
61XX	2-6-2T	GWR	70	65
64XX	0-6-0PT	GWR	40	22
68XX 'Grange'	4-6-0	GWR	80	77
6959 'Modified Hall'	4-6-0	GWR	32	71
72XX	2-8-2T	GWR	54	54
74XX	0-6-0PT	GWR	35	37
78XX 'Manor'	4-6-0	GWR	20	30
81XX	2-6-2T	GWR	10	7

Class	Wheel Arrangement	Origin	Number in Class 1948	1961
90XX 'Dukedog'	4-4-0	GWR	27	—
94XX	0-6-0PT	GWR	10	154
30XX 'ROD'*	2-8-0	ROD	32	—
—	0-4-0ST	YTW	1	—
—	0-4-2ST	Corris	1	—
—	0-4-2ST	Corris	1	—
†	0-6-0T	WCPR	1	—
—	2-6-2T	VoR	3	3
—	0-6-2T	BMR	13	—
—	0-6-0T	CMDPR	2	—
—	0-6-0T	RR	49	—
—	0-6-0T	RR	7	—
—	0-6-2T	Cardiff	1	—
—	0-6-0T	Cardiff	4	—
—	0-4-0ST	Cardiff	1	1
—	0-6-2T	PTR	1	—
—	0-6-2T	TVR	95	—
—	0-6-0T	TVR	3	—
—	0-6-2T	Barry	16	—
—	0-6-0T	Barry	1	—
—	0-6-0ST	LMMR	1	—
—	0-6-0T	ADR	3	—
—	2-6-2T	ADR	2	—
—	0-4-0ST	PM	4	1
—	0-6-0T	WLR	2	—
—	0-6-0	Cambrian	11	—
—	0-4-0ST	SHT	6	—
—	0-6-0ST	SHT	3	—
—	2-4-0	MSWJR	3	—
—	0-6-0T	WCR	1	—
—	0-6-0T	BPGVR	6	—
—	0-6-0T	BPGVR	7	—
Number of classes:			73	32
Number of locomotives:			3,777	2,499

*See also ex-LNER Class O4.
†See also ex-LBSCR Class A1X.

Key:

ADR	Alexandra Dock Railway
Barry	Barry Railway
BMR	Brecon & Merthyr Railway
BPGVR	Burry Port & Gwendraeth Valley Railway
BR	British Railways
Cambrian	Cambrian Railways
Cardiff	Cardiff Railway
CMDPR	Cleobury Mortimer & Ditton Priors Railway
Corris	Corris Railway
LMMR	Llanelli & Mynydd Mawr Railway
MSWJR	Midland & South Western Junction Railway
PM	Powesland & Mason
PTR	Port Talbot Railway
ROD	Royal Ordnance Department
RR	Rhymney Railway
SHT	Swansea Harbour Trust
TVR	Taff Vale Railway
VoR	Vale of Rheidol Railway
WLR	Welshpool & Llanfair Railway
WCPR	Weston, Cleveland & Portishead Railway
WCR	Whitland & Cardigan Railway
YTW	Ystalyfera Tin Works

Ex-War Department classes:

Class	Wheel Arrangement	Origin	Number in Class 1948	1961
WD	2-8-0	WD	499	730
WD	2-10-0	WD	—	23
Number of classes:			*1	2
Number of locomotives:			*499	753

*See also ex-LNER Class O7.

Class	Wheel Arrangement	Origin	Number in Class 1948	Number in Class 1961
British Railways Standard Classes:				
9F	2-10-0	BR	—	251
8P	4-6-2	BR	—	1
7P6F 'Britannia'	4-6-2	BR	—	55
6P5F 'Clan'	4-6-2	BR	—	10
5MT	4-6-0	BR	—	172
4MT	4-6-0	BR	—	80
4MT	2-6-0	BR	—	115
3MT	2-6-0	BR	—	20
2MT	2-6-0	BR	—	65
4MT	2-6-4T	BR	—	155
3MT	2-6-0	BR	—	65
2MT	2-6-2T	BR	—	30
Number of classes:			—	12
Number of locomotives:			—	999

SUMMARY

Railway	Number of Classes 1948	Number of Classes 1961	Number of Locomotives 1948	Number of Locomotives 1961
LNER	146	55	6,424	2,520
LMS	112	64	7,805	4,862
SR	87	39	1,810	782
GWR	73	32	3,777	2,499
WD	1	2	499	753
BR	—	12	—	999
Totals	419	204	20,315	12,415

	1948	1961
Average number of locomotives per class:	48.4	60.9

Summary of Motive Power Depots 1950 and 1961

Region	Number of depots 1950	Number of depots 1961
Eastern	50	32
North Eastern	32	35
London Midland	119	93
Scottish	44	42
Southern	37	26
Western	62	60
Total	344	288

All the above were depots having an allocation of steam locomotives. The summary excludes sub-depots.

Above:

The Great Eastern 'Claud Hamilton' 4-4-0s were good lookers. No 62548 was portrayed at March shed in April 1958. *T. B. Owen/Colour-Rail BRE562*

Top:

Ex-Great Central 'D11' 4-4-0 No 62663 *Prince Albert* leaves the now closed Sheffield Victoria station in September 1958 with a local service. *P. J. Hughes/Colour-Rail BRE292*

The graceful lines of a Drummond 'Greyhound' are exemplified by 'T9' 4-4-0 No 30120 posing at Eastleigh depot in 1957. *Colour-Rail BRS22*

Even in the standardisation atmosphere of the 1950s some livery variations did appear. Otherwise this smart ex-Great Northern 0-6-0ST No 68846 (Class J52) would have been plain black. *W. Potter/Colour-Rail BRE409*

Left:

The GWR 'Dukedogs' were basically 'Bulldog' chassis carrying 'Duke' type boilers. As such they were the last 4-4-0s to survive in Western Region service. No 9015 takes a local passenger train for Machynlleth near Llandre in August 1958. *T. B. Owen/Colour-Rail BRW501*

Left:

The Midland Railway's influence on the London, Tilbury & Southend Railway's locomotives is clear from this view of LTSR 4-4-2T No 41978 at Shoeburyness depot in 1956, near the end of its life. *T. B. Owen/Colour-Rail BRM699*

Below:

Designed specifically to negotiate the sharp curves at Southampton docks, Adams' 'B4' 0-4-0Ts of the LSWR were quite strong little machines. No 30083 poses at Eastleigh. *Colour-Rail BRS4*

Above:
The smallest ex-Great Western passenger tanks were the '14XX' class, of which No 1421 is pausing at Culmstock with the single coach 12.09pm to Tiverton Junction. This charming scene was photographed in November 1962.
P. W. Gray/Colour-Rail BRW452

Below:
An ex-North British Railway Class J83 0-6-0T, No 68474, tugs a few wagons into Edinburgh's Waverley station.
J. G. Wallace/Colour-Rail SC436

Above:
**Small engines often had to work hard. The ex-SECR 'R1'
class 0-6-0Ts which were used to haul and bank boat trains
up the steep grade from Folkestone Harbour to the junction
were flogged unmercifully on this duty. This one was
pictured at Dover Priory shed in July 1959.** *Colin Boocock*

Left:
**Another group of ancient engines that worked hard right
up to the end of their lives was the Midland '1F' 0-6-0T class
which was hired to the ironworks at Staveley. No 41708
heads a mixed train of wagons in 1963.** *Colin Boocock*

Left:
**Aberdeen harbour was shunted by four small 0-4-2Ts from
the former GNSR, like No 68192 which was still there in
1959, but had gone by the summer of 1960.**
Don Beecroft/Colour-Rail SC445

2 Dimensions of Principal Classes

Class	Weight (tons)	Boiler pressure (lb/sq in)	Cylinders: number and size	Driving wheels	Tractive effort (lb/ft)
8P					
BR '8P'	101	250	(3) 18×28in	6ft 2in	39,080
LM 'Coronation'	105	250	(4) 16.5×28in	6ft 9in	40,000
LM 'Princess'	104	250	(4) 16.25×28in	6ft 6in	40,285
ER 'A1'	104	250	(3) 19×26in	6ft 8in	37,400
ER 'A4'	102	250	(3) 18.5×26in	6ft 8in	35,455
SR Rebuilt 'Merchant Navy'	98	250	(3) 18×24in	6ft 2in	33,495
WR 'King'	89	250	(4) 16.25×28in	6ft 6in	40,285
7P					
BR '7MT'	94	250	(2) 20×28in	6ft 2in	32,150
ER 'A3'	96	220	(3) 19×26in	6ft 8in	32,910
SR 'WC'/'BB'	86/90	250	(3) 16.1×24in	6ft 2in	27,715
ER 'V2'	93	220	(3) 18.5×26in	6ft 2in	33,730
LM 'Royal Scot'	93	250	(3) 18×26in	6ft 9in	33,150
WR 'Castle'	80	225	(4) 16×26in	6ft 8.5in	31,625
SR 'Lord Nelson'	84	220	(4) 16.5×26in	6ft 7in	33,510
6P					
BR 'Clan'	87	225	(2) 19.5×28in	6ft 2in	27,520
LM 'Jubilee'	80	225	(3) 17×26in	6ft 9in	26,610
WR 'County'	77	250	(2) 18.5×30in	6ft 3in	28,240
5MT					
BR '5MT'	76	225	(2) 19×28in	6ft 2in	26,120
LM '5MT'	72/75	225	(2) 18.5×28in	6ft 0in	25,455
ER 'B1'	71	225	(2) 20×26in	6ft 2in	26,880
SR 'N15'	82	200	(2) 20.5×28in	6ft 7in	25,320
WR 'Hall'	75/76	225	(2) 18.5×30in	6ft 0in	27,275
WR 'Grange'	74	225	(2) 18.5×30in	5ft 8in	28,875
WR 'Manor'	69	225	(2) 18×30in	5ft 8in	27,340
4MT					
BR 4-6-0	69	225	(2) 18×28in	5ft 8in	25,100
BR 2-6-0	59	225	(2) 17.5×26in	5ft 3in	24,170
LM 2-6-0	59	225	(2) 17.5×26in	5ft 3in	24,170
WR 43XX	62/65	200	(2) 18.5×30in	5ft 8in	25,670
SR 'N'	61	200	(2) 19×28in	5ft 6in	26,035
4MT Tank					
BR	89	225	(2) 18×28in	5ft 8in	25,100
LM Fairburn	85	200	(2) 19.6×26in	5ft 9in	24.670
ER 'L1'	90	225	(2) 20×26in	5ft 2in	32,080
WR 61XX	79	225	(2) 18×30in	5ft 8in	27,340
8F/9F					
BR '9F'	87	250	(2) 20×28in	5ft 0in	39,670
WD 2-8-0	70	225	(2) 19×28in	4ft 8.5in	34,215
LM '8F'	72	225	(2) 18.5×28in	4ft 8.5in	32,440
ER 'O1'	73	225	(2) 20×26in	4ft 8in	35,520
WR 28XX	76	225	(2) 18.5×30in	4ft 7.5in	35,380
5F/4F					
ER 'J39'	58	180	(2) 20×26in	5ft 2in	25,665
SR 'Q1'	51	230	(2) 19×26in	5ft 1in	30,080
LM '4F'	49	175	(2) 20×26in	5ft 3in	24,555
3MT					
BR 2-6-0	57	200	(2) 17.4×26in	5ft 3in	21,490
WR 45XX	57/61	200	(2) 17×24in	4ft 7.5in	21,250
WR 2251	43	200	(2) 17.5×24in	5ft 2in	20,155
3MT Tank					
BR 2-6-2T	74	200	(2) 17.5×26in	5ft 3in	21,490
LM 2-6-2T	71/73	200	(2) 17.5×26in	5ft 3in	21,490
2MT					
BR 2-6-0	49	200	(2) 16.5×24in	5ft 0in	18,515
LM 2-6-0	47	200	(2) 16×24in	5ft 0in	17,410
2MT Tank					
BR 2-6-2T	63	200	(2) 16.5×24in	5ft 0in	18,515
LM 2-6-2T	63	200	(2) 16×24in	5ft 0in	17,410

At Polmadie depot, Glasgow, in September 1956 stands No 46118 *Royal Welch Fusilier* showing off the graceful form of the 'Rebuilt Scots'. *J. G. Wallace/Colour-rail SC338*

A nice clean '9F' shows off its bulk at South Pelaw while hauling coal hoppers for Consett in July 1966.
J. G. Dewing/Colour-Rail BRE148

Top:
Near the top end of the dimensional scale were the LMS 'Princess Royal' 4-6-2s. No 46203 *Princess Margaret Rose* stands at Carlisle Citadel station between duties.
Colin Boocock

Above:
The LMS 'Jubilees' totalled 191 locomotives, of which No 45675 *Hardy*, seen here at Willesden depot, is a splendid example. *Colin Boocock*

Above:
No 31790 was one of the original SECR 2-6-4T 'River' class that had been rebuilt as Class U 2-6-0s by the Southern Railway following the Sevenoaks derailment. In July 1959 it was photographed at Tonbridge shortly after a works overhaul. *Colin Boocock*

Left:
In June 1950 one of the last GW 'Saint' 4-6-0s to be given an overhaul, No 2934 *Butleigh Court*, was photographed at Swindon shed. *T. B. Owen/Colour-Rail BRW417*

Left:
Urie 'Arthur' 4-6-0 No 30742 *Camelot* still carried SR malachite green livery at Eastleigh in 1950 though lettered and numbered by BR. *T. B. Owen/Colour-Rail BRS389*

Ribblehead Viaduct supports Class 5 No 44680 and its up freight, backed by snow-capped Whernside in April 1967.
D. Smith/Colour-Rail BRM722